The Cult of MAMMON

Critiquing the Prosperity Gospel and the Underpinning Theology of the Word of Faith Movement

APPRAISALS

"The book is well researched and portrays an accurate picture of those who peddle the prosperity gospel."

Dr Reuben van Rensburg
Principal of the South African Theological Seminary (SATS): 2000-2018
Current Project Director of Re-Forma www.re-forma.global

"The book is such a good read. Very rich and informative on the truth. It could ruffle some feathers but arguably with the intent to make them repent. After all, only the Truth will set us free."
Dr Tarwireyi Kurisa MBChB, MMed
Dip. in Biblical Studies (Zimbabwe)

"*Mammon* is well written and thoroughly researched. I found Sylvester's insight to be deep and revealing. I would recommend this book to anyone who has doubts about religious charlatans and those taking advantage of vulnerable Christians. The answers to many questions contained in *Mammon* are shocking! Pastor Sylvester, thanks so much for delving into such a difficult subject and I pray God's blessings for any new work you put your hands to."
Steve Zimmerman
Professor of Academic Development at Divinity College International
Director of Cape Bible Seminary (South Africa)
Author of *My Brother Philemon*

"This work is much needed and greatly appreciated for our times such as with the spirit of the prosperity age continuing to deceive the masses. Brother Tonderai has wasted no time to show with biblical precision and carefully presented exegesis to this subject. The many links and resources will also prove a great help to further the quest in understanding this movement, God has greatly used him to articulate and those laypeople who want to further their study to teach others trapped in its web of deception. This is a necessary and important add to the Christian's library for years to come."
Minister McKinley Caughman
Reformed Theologist, Atlanta Georgia

"Dr Sylvester has taken a necessary apologetic stand against a growing populist Word of Faith Movement in the area of money. Well researched and relevant data allows the reader to realize the margin of error and level of confusion brought about by the ever evolving and intentionally misleading teachings on this subject matter that has become rife in our time.

This reading resource comes at an opportune time, raising a sound Christocentric viewpoint in the midst of many other so-called biblical teachings. Brother Sylvester's writing is a call for those caught up in heretic teachings on money to repent and those seeking Truth to be set free. This book is must-read."

Pastor Mbongeni Simelane (Eswatini) BSc. (Hon) Const. Management
Master's in Ministry (Undergraduate)

"I've known Dr Sylvester Tonderai Faravadya all my life: he's my bookish brother – the last born in our family. Our upbringing taught us that God can mould character through challenges. We see the amazing hand of God especially in his life. At a time when people can be in ministry for fame or fortune, Pastor Sylvester's principled and uncompromising approach keenly focuses on the glory of God. It is even evident in this book that he calls a spade a spade. Clearly his depth and diligence in researching even in this book confirms his raging passion in Theology that I witnessed since he was a teenager! He goes all the way to unearth evidence on the origins of Mammonism. Hosea 4:6-7 says my people are perishing because of lack of knowledge. We are witnessing people being misled, manipulated, and robbed in broad daylight by some so-called men of God. Hence the Body of Christ urgently needed a book such as this!"
Tendai Faravadya
Pastor and Recording Gospel Musician (Zimbabwe)

"It is a great pleasure to have an opportunity to taste this pot before you dish it out. I salute you for standing firm in truth on behalf of God – not for people against God! ... You are teaching us to go back to the original purpose of worshipping God. Churches and preachers should indeed focus on the transformation of the soul in order to express righteousness through reverencing God and loving the brethren, rather than pursuing stratagems of selfish enrichment. We now have motivational speakers who are nothing but parasites using the Bible for their self-enrichment by pretending to be messengers of God as well as disguised fortune-tellers misleading and taking advantage of the poor and vulnerable members in the pretext of comforting.
The book is sending a strong message to the world and all centres of faith in the Christian society to repent from this evil spirit found in our churches. This is cruel and a blasphemy to God when we turn into wolves in sheep's clothing because of money. If indeed we are messengers of God, then the Gospel is supposed to be free. Christianity should have regulations according to the will of God so that the faith does not become an open field for anyone to play his or her personal games."
Bishop Sisa Mpambaniso
The Twelve Apostles in Cape Town, South Africa

"This book is a tremendous resource for anyone wishing to understand the transgressions of this dangerous movement and many of the big-name heretics who push it. The church must stand strong in proclaiming the true gospel and our eternal heavenly hope in order to avoid falling prey to the temptations of the feelings oriented, me first movement that is temporal in scope."
Ekkie Tepsupornchai
The Master's Seminary M. Div.
Senior Pastor of Western Avenue Baptist Church, California

(Appraisals continue ... Back Cover)

All the glory to God, as I dedicate this book
to two particular angels of my life,
who exemplified good stewardship
in their unshakeable faith,
unquestionable integrity,
impeccable industry,
cheerful generosity,
unmatched sacrifices,
and gracious humility:

My Mother
Ronia Faravadya nee Mpedziswa
(25 December 1951 – 27 August 2011)

&

My Grandma

Ellinella Kurisa nee Hunidzarira
(30 June 1938 –)

CONTENTS

PREFACE

Much has been said and written about the prosperity 'gospel', to such a large extent that the effort of this book could just be a drop in the ocean. I grew up in a bigamous family that could be classified among the poorest of the poor insomuch that 'being blind' was just an icing on the cake (I was born with a cataract that covered my right pupil and kids would have fun days by calling me blind). Yet none of these setbacks would ultimately dissuade me from going to church. Church then meant the Gospel, preaching Christ that leads to repentance. And godly fellowship meant there was no classicism among the brethren.

Considering the dominance of the Word of Faith movement in the Christian media, my upbringing was exposed to the movement more than other facets of Christianity. Yet the more time God gave me to pore over the biblical and theological material, the more I started to question the movement's interpretation of Scripture. Constantly witnessing colleagues starting churches premised on prosperity preaching, numerous invitations to join prosperity preaching church leaderships as well as the mission field that gave me an opportunity to share the platform with diverse speakers at conferences are few factors that can demonstrate my familiarity with the subject at hand. Furthermore, the need for objectivity resulted in attending church services centralized on prosperity preaching, watching televised Word of Faith services, engaging Christians even from opposing viewpoints – including prosperity preachers – reading quite extensively on materials relevant to the subject as well as submitting the manuscript to a diversity of scholars and seminaries to be critiqued.

'Great minds discuss ideas; average minds discuss events; small minds discuss people'. The prime gist of this thesis is therefore to address the metaphysical grand ideas of the great minds of Word of Faith movement particularly in view of the prosperity gospel. Above all, this main thrust also evinces the standpoint of sound theology in the potency and objectiveness of the Bible. People are, therefore, discussed only in view of the ideologies they are presenting. Whenever possible, it is indeed imperative to be at peace with all men yet never at the expense of the Truth. I remember being turned down by a renowned Christian publisher for the reason that 'they do not expose famous Christians'! The intent of writing this rebuttal is neither mud-slinging nor fault-finding but a defence of the Gospel entrusted to the Church for its preservation and faithful proclamation.

The central motif of my theological expressions and ministration is the glory of God. I can do no other. To this end, I pray that God gets glory from this confutation.

Sylvester Tonderai Faravadya

Soli Deo Gloria

FOREWORD

The book is best summed up by the periscope, "Rather than being a message of self-denial (Matt. 16:24-26), the prosperity gospel is one of self-satisfaction, self-esteem, self-glorification which thrives in the self-help mass market."

In battle, it is always wise to "know your enemy." Satan is no longer fighting from without. Distorted theology is no longer simply at the gate. It has infiltrated the church and represents itself as proper doctrine, attracting thousands (if not millions) of desperate souls.

The cult of Mammon is pervasive. Although it began as a uniquely American form of self-gratification, it has been exported worldwide. Fed by the ubiquitous presence of social media and modern narcissism, the prosperity gospel has replaced orthodox Christianity in many church circles.

My own wife, the lovely Australian, was caught up in the Word of Faith scheme, spending years of her life at Rhema Bible School, absorbing the teaching of Kenneth Hagin. God has graciously delivered her from that school of error and the tool He used was proper doctrine and solid exegesis.

Sylvester Tonderai Faravadya has written a balanced critique of the movement, its history, its major players, and its theological underpinnings. Chapter three, "Prosperity Theology" is worth the price of admission.

And, knowing that the cure for wrong use is right use, Faravadya includes a proper biblical perspective on questions of giving, receiving, and properly supporting the advance of the gospel.

We, as the church of the living God, should be ever vigilant. Error takes no vacations. Satan still goes about like a roaring lion. And, from the beginning, our enemy has inspired people to doubt or question God's word. Manmade doctrine continues to be taught as though it were the very word of God. Books like Faravadya's push back against the veil of darkness, exposing error with the light of the gospel.

The time, effort, and zeal of the author are commendable. The research is accurate. And the conclusions are worthy of consideration.

Mammon is well worth the read.

Pastor Jim McClarty

Grace Christian Assembly, Smyrna, Tennessee

Author of 'By Grace Alone'

www.salvationbygrace.org

1. MAMMON!

"No one can serve two masters;
for either he will hate the one and love the other,
or else he will be loyal to the one and despise the other.
You cannot serve God and mammon." [1]

The noun *mammon* is derived from the Greek term "*mammonas*" and it has synonymic terms in Chaldean, Syriac, Aramaic, Hebrew, and Latin linguistics. Since the term Mammon is not only key to this critique but is central to its presentation as well, it is imperative to, at least, have a glimpse into the scholastic understanding of the term. Whereas English lexicons define *mammon* as gloss wealth or material avarice, *Strong's Exhaustive Concordance* describes *mammon* as being "of Chaldee origin (confidence, i.e., wealth, personified); *mammonas*, i.e., avarice (deified)." *Robertson's Word Pictures in the New Testament* further explains that "Mammon is a Chaldee, Syriac, and Punic word, like the Greek word [Plutus] for the money-god (or devil)" and *M. G. Easton's Bible Dictionary* also defines Mammon as "a Chaldee or Syriac word meaning 'wealth' or 'riches' (Luke 16:9-11); also, by personification, the god of riches (Matthew 6:24; Luke 16:9-11)."

Dr Thomas Constable comments on Matthew 6:24 thus: "The choice between two masters is behind two treasures and the choice between two visions. 'Mammon' is the transliteration of the emphatic form of the Aramaic word *mamona*, meaning 'wealth' or 'property.' The root word *mn*, in both Hebrew and Aramaic, indicates something in which one places confidence. Here Jesus personified it and set it over against God as a competing object of confidence. Jesus presented God and Mammon as two slave owners, masters." [2] Mammon is mentioned four times in the New Testament [3] and Matthew 6:19-34 is closely paralleled in Luke 12:22-34 and 16:1-31 where the contexts make a sharp contrast between the values of earthly and heavenly treasures. The contexts challenge one's ultimate allegiance for the desires of a person's heart, which are confirmed by what that person treasures. The contradistinction between God and Mammon is evinced by the fact that the former is a benevolent master, and the latter is a malevolent owner.

Whereas Luke 16:9 and 16:11 refer to Mammon as 'worldly resources', the Lord's stinging indictment of Mammonites in Matthew 6:24 and Luke 16:13 goes beyond the mere definition of Mammonism as relentless pursuance of wealth in all its material forms. He openly exposes Mammon to be the personified anti-God demon who deifies material wealth.

In essence, Mammon is a money-god that is central to materialism. Indeed, history is replete with evidence that diehard adherents to the occult will do anything for their deity, to the extent of deceiving, blaspheming, manipulating and even killing. In his book *Neither Poverty nor Riches: A Biblical Theology of Possessions*, a book very relevant to the subject at hand, Dr Craig Blomberg points out aright that "it is arguable that materialism is the single biggest competitor with authentic Christianity for the hearts and souls of millions in our world today, including many in the visible church."[4]

Mammonism is indeed the pursuit of great wealth. Yet "the principle of materialism is in inevitable conflict with the kingship of God."[5] Professor Randolph Tasker, who specialized in New Testament exegesis, noted that "men cannot *serve* (i.e., 'be slaves of') *God* and mammon (Knox 'money') at once, for single ownership and full-time service are of the essence of slavery."[6]A Mammonite or Mammonist is a person devoted to the acquisition of wealth or the service of Mammon. Therefore, to put it bluntly, mammonizing Christian leaders on a quest to fraud the naive and Mammonish congregates are demonic because Mammon is the ardent desire for wealth personified as an evil spirit. Mammonization therefore should be rebuked and exposed!

MAMMONISM IN THE OLD TESTAMENT

People who follow God for the goodies that He can provide, rather than who He is, in essence simply use God as a footnote to their carnal desires. Lot walked by the greediness of sight when he was occasioned to choose by Abraham, then Abram. He gave a blind eye to the sinful lifestyle of the Sodomites in choosing the fertile plains of the Jordan. No wonder his wife, having sipped into the culture of Sodom, could not get enough of the Mammon of the place, and obeying the Lord's command to safety weighed less in her heart than her crazy love for materialism. Lot's character clearly contrasted with the moral strength of Abraham who, after rescuing his enslaved nephew, did not only flatly turn down the shrewd request of the king of Sodom for human capital but the sinful Mammon of Sodom as well lest the Sodomites would have claimed credit and bragging rights over his prosperity. Discerningly, Abram would rather give the tithe to Melchizedek – king of peace and righteousness with an eternal priesthood and neither beginning nor end! Lot's association with Sodom was overwhelming inasmuch as after being redeemed he nonetheless returned to dwell and conduct business in the city! Breaking the Israelites' command to marry amongst their kind, Lot's daughters were even engaged to be married to Sodomites! So overpowering was Lot's obsession with the Mammon of the city that had it not been for the intercession of Abraham, Lot could have perished in the impending judgement of God upon the sin city. Seeing his hesitation to leave behind his wealth, position, and associations, the angels literally had to seize him and his family away from doom.[7]

Whilst money and material wealth indubitably have a pivotal role in this fallen world, in the Kingdom of God, material wealth cannot be used as a measure of God's blessings lest rich tyrants and immoral executives would misrepresent the biblical significance of blessings. In the Old Testament, God's intent was to illustrate the nature of His kingdom by distinguishing Israel from the pagan nations.[8] Hence when they opted for a human king instead of His kingship, they were fundamentally choosing Mammon over God inasmuch as Samuel's prophecy confirmed that Israel would become just like any other nation in governance: lands were taxed, sons were conscripted into the army and daughters became concubines, cooks, and bakers of the royal family.

Deifying money violates the First and Tenth Commandments for the reason that a believer should not have anything to worship but God. And covetousness explains the desire to be avaricious.[9] Whereas Moses would rather leave the Mammon of Pharaoh and share in the sufferings of God's people because he "esteemed the reproach of Christ greater riches than the treasures in Egypt,"[10] later in the Old Testament the prophets would highlight Mammon worship with the erection and worship of expensive idols made of silver and gold by the selfsame people of God.[11] God had to remind especially the affluent Israelites who had returned from the Babylonian captivity that the very silver and gold was His! Hence the glory of the latter Temple would be incomparable inasmuch as, in three days, Christ, the eternal Temple, would resurrect and ascend in glory.[12] Are some Christian leaders not falling into the same trap by fleecing the flock to 'sow' into the construction of highfalutin infrastructure as if that is how God is centrally worshipped?

Israel would turn to God when they were in need, yet when they had materially prospered and their now sleek and pampered wives were 'fattened like the cows of Bashan', they were quick to build for themselves pagan shrines and set up Asherah poles on every high hill and under every green tree.[13] Since Asherah, or Ashtoreth, was considered the mistress of Baal and her worship glorified sex, shrine prostitutes could be found throughout the land. Even during the golden age of Israel's material prosperity under the wise King Solomon, gods such as Baal, Molech, and Chemosh were worshipped because, at the end of the day, the idolaters preferred Mammon over the only God. Only during the reign of Jeroboam IIcould Israel near such dizzying heights of material prosperity. Yet this prosperity had much to do with military strength and administrative policies that enriched the rich and exploited the poor insomuch as the son of Jehoash was hardly devoted to God.[14] Ironically, Mammon could neither satisfy with lasting happiness nor save the Mammonites from the wrath of God over the exploitation of the greedy who went as far as using gold and silver to mould vile idols.[15]

MAMMONISM IN THE NEW TESTAMENT

Likewise in the New Testament, the Epistle of James for instance has a poignant condemnation of believers who prostitute themselves with the corrupt and self-centred system of this fallen world by prioritizing materialism over spiritual wellbeing. Hence, there is no favourable response to their prayers because they ask amiss.[16] The Apostle John explains the Mammonish system of the world, its temporality as well as its relationship to the Kingdom of God thus: "For all that is in the world, the lust of the flesh, the lust of the eyes, and the pride of life is not of the Father but is of the world. And the world is passing away, and the lust of it; but he who does the will of God abides forever."[17]

Mammon is indeed the idol of self-indulgence, self-gratification, self-fulfilment, and self-glorification. Scripture, particularly in Revelation 18-19, could not arguably depict any better the stark contrast between the corrupt and corrupting treasures of Mammonism and the eternal treasures of the Kingdom of God. Babylon, in this preclusion to the imminence of Christ, represents the Mammonish whoredom which includes religious people probably at a catch 22 in choosing between God and Mammon! Furthermore, even the legendary mark of the beast, if read at face value, entails commerce inasmuch as those loyal to Christ are persecuted and prohibited from participating in business unless they renege on their faith. The kings of the earth who influenced and intoxicated the harlotry religion will stand aside in shock at the rapid judgement of the temple of Mammon by the righteous Judge. It is noteworthy that the influence of the religion of Mammon was so overwhelming insomuch that its demise had a direct impact on the commerce of the nations that enjoyed and benefited from this illicit association. Even its expensive citadels, mass communication infrastructure, state of the art musical instruments, visual equipment, and light displays that had been used to manipulate emotions with carnal genres, are shattered to smithereens. The elect of God rejoices at the judgement of the materialism machinery that had fine-tuned expertise in the character assassination of the servants of God who upheld sound doctrine and rebuked the mammonization of the visible church.[18]

The *Theological Dictionary of the New Testament* comments: "This spatial separation from Babylon not only expresses the horror they [the 'kings'] feel at its sudden and unexpected destruction; it also reflects their attempt to distance themselves from a judgment they deserve to share."[19] Even Wikipedia points out that writers such as John Milton in '*Paradise Lost*', Edmund Spencer in his poem '*The Faerie Queene*', and Dante

Alighieri in the famous poem '*The Divine Comedy*' used personifications of Mammon to show the insidious nature of materialism and its seductive qualities to humanity.

Scripture speaks in unmistakable terms on the dangers of materialistic lifestyles and the illusiveness of trying to own Mammon.[20] Satan, having saved his best bait for last, promised to give Mammon to our Lord, who sharply rebuked the Tempter and unequivocally pointed out that only God, not the idol of materialism, is to be worshipped and served.[21] And Professor Tasker again commented: "Jesus was in effect tempted to subscribe to the diabolical doctrine that the end justifies the means; that, so long as He obtained universal sovereignty in the end, it mattered not how that sovereignty was reached"[22] If believers today love and pursue what the world loves and pursues, how different are we then to the Mammonites?

MAMMON IN OUR SOCIETIES

Mammonism occurs when material wealth controls peoples' lives. Mammon is essentially at work when social structures and social gatherings indicate where one stays. Mammon is at work when one deliberately puts hindering measures in place to determine how far the other can go in life regardless of the exponential ability. The one who gives another working hours and a corresponding salary is substantially determining the time the worker has to self as well as the lifestyle the worker is going to have. Indeed one's acceptance or rejection corresponds to one's social standing especially in view of material wealth[23] because Mammonites quantify life according to the material wealth in one's possession.[24] Yet in so doing God has less or no value in their life inasmuch as no one can serve masters of conflicting ideologies.[25] In a Mammonish society, a corrupt person's riches are more welcome than a poor person's integrity.[26]

Luke 16 deals to a great extent with material possessions as is evinced in the Parable of the Shrewd Manager and the Parable of the Rich Man and Lazarus. The former shows that non-believers follow the system of Mammon in such a way that believers should emulate their diligence in investment by investing with such prudence in the Kingdom of God. Note that it does not teach that the believers should follow the Mammonites in the system of this world the way the Pharisees, who were also in attendance, were rebuked for. The essential lesson of the parable is highlighted by the Lord in His conclusion when He evinces His philosophy that money is temporal and should never be used as a taskmaster but as a tool for good purposes that brings us friends and, above all, purposes for the Kingdom of God such as in the missionary field where souls are saved. He even questions that if we fail to be diligent with material wealth, how then can we be trusted with the true riches of the Kingdom? The Parable of the Rich Man and Lazarus is another ostensible indictment to the Pharisees who are illustrated in the parable by the rich man and his brothers. Pharisees were known for showy piety as well as opulent lifestyles. This is how our fallen world operates but it should not be so in the kingdom ruled by Christ where God calls the downtrodden His very people.[27] Hence monetary ethics established by Christ were antithetical to the norms of His day.

While joy is an inward characteristic of a believer that is not determined by outward circumstances, the happiness of the Mammonites is directly tied to their wealth. Sociology Professor Robert Wuthnow, who was project director on a national survey on Religious and Economic Beliefs and Values, remarked: "Jesus warned his followers of the impossibility of serving God and Mammon. Are those who claim to be his followers today, then, defying this warning by trying to be spiritual and yet being unwilling to detach from materialistic pursuits? Or perhaps we have found a way to get beyond these ancient tensions, living in material abundance and yet keeping our eyes fixed steadfastly on the sacred. Perhaps American religion even encourages us in some subtle way to amass worldly riches. Or perhaps our faith has become so narrowly defined that it seldom pricks our conscience when pocketbook issues are at stake."[28]

And scholar Martin Hengel aptly remarks: "Jesus was not interested in any new theories about the rightness or wrongness of possessions in themselves, about the origin of the property or its better distribution; rather he adopted the same scandalously free and untrammelled attitude towards the property, as to the powers of the state, the alien Roman rule, and its Jewish confederates. The imminence of the kingdom of God robs all these things of their power de facto, for in it 'many that are first will be last, and the last first' (Mark 10:31;Matthew 19:30, 20:16; Luke 13:30). Of course, Jesus attacks mammon with the utmost severity where it has captured men's hearts, because this gives it demonic character by which it blinds men's eyes to God's will—in concrete terms, to their neighbour's needs. Mammon is worshipped wherever men long for riches, are tied to riches, keep on increasing their possessions, and want to dominate because of them."[29]

In essence, eternal life matters more than our material needs and wants. Material provision has value, but never at the expense of eternal treasure. Money has the power to place our integrity on the line therefore it must never be seen as an end in itself. The very loving and provident God who created everything can surely sustain His creation. Failure to maintain integrity on earthly treasures speaks volumes on a heart so corrupt that it cannot have integrity on heavenly treasures, as the Parable of the Rich Man and Lazarus highlights, inasmuch as Pharisaical theology alleged that material wealth was evidence that one was faithful to the Law. Another scholar Stanley Hauerwas comments, "Possessed by possessions, we discover that we cannot will our way free of our possessions. But if we can be freed, our attention may be grasped by that which is so true, so beautiful: we discover we have been dispossessed. To seek first the righteousness of the kingdom of God is to discover that that for which we seek is given, not achieved."[30]

Money is not evil in itself inasmuch as it improves commerce. Otherwise without money civilization is reduced to Stone Age barter trade and barbarism. The bone of contention is the lust for money – the kind of love that enslaves to such an extent people do anything for money. Theology Professor Wayne Grudem expresses the point thus: "So money is simply a tool for our use, and we can rightly thank God that in his wisdom he ordained that we would invent it and use it. It is simply a 'medium of exchange,' something that makes voluntary exchanges possible. It is a commodity ... that is legally established as an exchangeable equivalent of all other commodities, such as goods and services, and is used as a measure of their comparative values on the market."[31] And professor of New Testament at the Augustana Hochschule, Neuendettelsau in Germany, Wolfgang Stegemann's *The Gospel and the Poor's* concise contemporary application of Luke 16:1-9 is spot on: "We affluent Christians, too, can make friends for ourselves by means of unrighteous mammon. We can become poorer in a purposeful way by giving away part of our wealth to benefit the poorest people of the world."[32]

2.   THE AMERICAN DREAM

Professor of Sociology of Religion at Vanderbilt, Sandra Barnes, notes that "Some writers contend that Prosperity theology and Word of Faith theology are not the same. However, the general consensus appears to suggest that proponents of the latter group embrace the general tenets of Prosperity theology."[33] In fact, Prosperity 'Gospel' and the Word of Faith movement are so interlinked that they are fundamentally one and the same. Hence the Word of Faith movement is also called the Seed Faith movement. The various names by which the prosperity movement is known also helps in defining it: Word-Faith, Faith Movement, New Apostolic Reformation, prosperity theology, health and wealth gospel, seed faith, seed faith theology, hyperfaith, name it and claim it, blab it and grab it, believe it and receive it, positive speech, positive confession theology, pop gospel, the gospel of success, gospel of excess or gospel of greed. Regardless of its prominence, both the terms 'Prosperity Gospel' and 'Health and Wealth Gospel' are misnomers inasmuch as there is fundamentally nothing prosperous, healthy, or wealthy regarding heresy. Gospel? This is not the Gospel but another – a false gospel, a heresy, a damnable heresy. It is blasphemy because it corrupts the attributes of God by presenting Him as buyable. Hence the term Prosperity Movement is more befitting. It is more than a fake gospel. A false gospel cannot save anyone. It is bankrupt because its view of prosperity is essentially antithetical to the blessings of the Lord.

Concerning 'another' gospel, the Apostle Paul charged: "I am astonished that you are so quickly deserting the one who called you by the grace of Christ and are turning to a different gospel—which is really no gospel at all. Evidently, some people are throwing you into confusion and are trying to pervert the gospel of Christ. But even if we or an angel from heaven should preach a gospel other than the one we preached to you, let him be eternally condemned! As we have already said, so now I say again: If anybody is preaching to you a gospel other than what you accepted, let him be eternally condemned!"[34]

WORD OF FAITH MOVEMENT

Whereas it is complex to precisely pinpoint the origin of a movement, according to records, the prosperity movement in its modern form was birthed, bred, shaped and defined in America in the nineteenth century and is essentially a product of several philosophies. The Word of Faith movement has deep roots in the charismatic movement. It is essentially a neo-Pentecostal contemporary subculture. Ever since the Roman Catholic rector Dennis J. Bennett and his parishioners declared in 1960 that they had been baptized in the Holy Ghost and could now speak in tongues, the Charismatic movement did not only start flourishing but even resulted in ecumenical fellowships between Catholic and Protestant Charismatics. Whereas the Charismatic movement was an essential catalyst in the shift from outdoor Pentecostal revivals to indoor gatherings which, to a good extent, set the foundation for the modern-day megachurch trend, it should be pointed out that, not all Charismatics or Pentecostals subscribe to the prosperity movement. For instance, Professor Gordon Fee is a Pentecostal pastor who refutes the prosperity 'gospel.' Christian theologian Robert M. Bowman Jr's book, *The Word-Faith Controversy*, is recommendable because, as pointed out, not all Pentecostal churches subscribe to prosperity theology.

Kenneth Copeland is certainly a prominent figure of the Word of Faith movement, but Kenneth Hagin Sr is widely considered to be the very father of the movement. Even his son, Kenneth Hagin Jr, conceded: "People frequently credit my father, Kenneth E. Hagin, with being the 'father' of the so-called faith movement. However, as he points out, it's nothing new; it's just the preaching of the simple ageless gospel. But he has had a great effect on many of the well-known faith ministers of today. Almost every major faith ministry of the United States has been influenced by his ministry."[35] Nevertheless, the striking similarities between Kenneth Hagin Sr and E. W. Kenyon's work have strongly been argued that the former plagiarized on the latter. Even Ruth Kenyon Houseworth, daughter of Kenyon, stated: "They've [the Faith teachers] all copied from my Dad [E. W. Kenyon]. They have changed it a little bit and added their own touch ... but they couldn't change the wording. The Lord gave him [Kenyon] words and phrases. He coined them. They cannot put it in any other words ... It's very difficult for some people to be big enough to give credit to somebody else."[36]

By dissecting the theologies which underpin the Word of Faith movement, a substantial number of ideologies can be identified which were instrumental in its formation and are the driving force behind its influence: New Thought metaphysics and positivism, Gnosticism, Pelagianism, sentimentalism, materialism, televangelism, pop culture celebrity lifestyle and, particularly in the Third World narrative, animism. Yet all these elements could not be as effective independently as they became unified under Christianity, especially considering the overwhelming following that the faith has. Considering the hocus pocus hotbed of syncretism that it is built upon, it is then no wonder that prosperity preaching has been very effective in affecting both the ignorant and the greedy.

Whereas metaphysical ideologies of the likes of Ralph Waldo Emerson, Emmanuel Swedenborg, and Helena Blavatsky laid the foundation, it was notably the mesmerist and forerunner of modern psychotherapy Phineas Parkhurst Quimby's secular New Thought that became prominent to such an extent that the likes of Ralph Waldo Trine, Mary Baker Eddy, and John Alexander Dowie ended up bringing the clairvoyance to church. Metaphysical religions claim that there is a link and transference of energy between the human mind and the spirit world. Therefore, believers are made to believe that they have the power to command and the material world obeys since God gave them dominion over His vast creation. Dr R. Albert Mohler Jr remarked "Quimby himself was a rather secular person. He offered a rather secular, positive thinking kind of worldview, but it was picked up by many others. Most famously, immediately in his interest, there was one of his patients who made this into an entire theological system. Her name was Mary Baker Eddy and she became the founder of what became known as Christian Science. A new thought movement so comprehensively new thought in its shape, that she denied the reality of death, sin, pain, and illness."[37]

Ironically, Eddy's Christian Science is neither Christian nor scientific and New Thought is nothing but mental magic! The role played by the likes of Essek William Kenyon and, later, Charles Fillmore was to harmonize neo-Pentecostalism with New Thought ideology. In already such a whirlpool of ideologies, the schools of positive thinking of Robert Schuller and Norman Vincent Peale had to be added in. Interestingly, while Norman Vincent Peale was a former Methodist minister, both Schuller and Peale were ordained in the Reformed Church in America. It is noteworthy that the fusion of New Thought and positive thinking paved the way to the modern-day trend of fusing Biblical counselling with secular psychology. Further, add the 1980s boom in televangelism plus the global impact of America's pop culture, the modern-day trend of charismatic megachurches as well as celebrity preachers then you have an explosive and magnetic subculture.

It came as no surprise when Trinity Broadcasting Network (TBN) became the home of prosperity preachers because its owners, Jan and Paul Crouch, are prosperity 'preachers' themselves! Harrison House became a home of prosperity paperbacks because it was owned by none other than the son-in-law of Kenneth Hagin, Buddy Harrison! Indeed, the impact and contribution of the Rhema Bible Training Centre and Oral Roberts University towards the prosperity movement cannot be underrated considering that the two institutes heavily influenced tens of thousands of students with their founders' theologies. The students went on to become pastors of their own churches. And the official publication of Rhema Bible Training Centre is aptly called *Word of Faith* magazine. In fact, the Word of Faith movement is named after this publication by Hagin! Even African prosperity preacher David Oyedepo founded Word of Faith Bible Institute. The prosperity teaching then is fundamentally a product of the materialism of the American Dream, the metaphysics of the New Thought movement, and, particularly in Africa, a camouflaged dose of animism, capped with the excitement on steroids of the Charismatic movement which is undergirded by extra-biblical heresies being sold as a revelation – though they are nothing short of modern-day repackaged forms of Gnosticism.

David W. Jones, professor of Christian ethics, also pointed out the diversity of philosophies that made up the prosperity movement by stating: "While it is impossible to trace the prosperity gospel back to an exact starting point, there are at least three movements from which it draws its ideas. One is the experience-centred Christianity which was birthed in the mind of nineteenth-century theologian Friedrich Schleiermacher and has come to fruition in the form of the twentieth-century Charismatic movement. A second philosophy that gave rise to the prosperity gospel was the 'positive thinking' school of Norman Vincent Peale. Indeed, scholar Harvey Cox wrote concerning the prosperity gospel that 'it owed much to the 'positive thinking' of the late Norman Vincent Peale' ... The third modern movement that has influenced the prosperity gospel is simply the 'American dream,' or materialism."[38]

PROSPERITY GOSPEL

Prosperity gospel claims that if a believer obeys God and maintains a positive confession, then God will bless that person with health, wealth and happiness in this life. Whereas the prosperity gospel expresses itself in diverse forms and emanates from multiple streams, its distinct themes remain health, wealth, and positivism. Hence, a prosperity preacher may not necessarily focus intensely on preaching about money but health in a Word of Faith manner that claims sickness to be an indication that one is outside the favour of God. One can preach one key theme of the prosperity message more prominently than the others, yet all the three key themes are essentially interlinked. Churches and ministries that fall under the prosperity movement, while they have differences, are characteristically identifiable by the core set of beliefs they share centralized on the motto: 'God wants to bless you!' Again Professor Barnes explains: "The Faith Movement is a mélange of elements drawn and recombined anew from a variety of traditions, including Evangelicalism, neo-Pentecostalism, and more important, New Thought metaphysics. Three basic points form the core of the Faith Movement. These are the principle of knowing who you are in Christ; the practice of positive confession (and positive mental attitudes); and a worldview that emphasizes material prosperity and physical health as the divine right of every Christian."[39]

Virtually all prosperity gospel preachers are non-denominational because not being affiliated to a denomination gives them more latitude to be independent ministers unaccountable to a hierarchy. Indeed, while churches and ministries within the Word of

Faith movement associate and fellowship for spiritual mentorship and ordination, they are essentially autonomous and pan denominational. The independency goes insofar as there is neither hierarchical structure of plural leadership nor an overall governing body because that is the key reason all prosperity preachers left traditional churches – to set up independent ministries. For instance, the Creflo Dollar's Ministerial Association (CDMA) outlines that rather than fearing accountability, investigations, or disciplinary actions from governing bodies that oversee churches or outreach ministries, CDMA only prefers to complement a church or ministry's assignment by providing expertise and leaving judgment to God.[40] It looks like we are no longer our brother's keepers anymore. Though it ultimately failed, in the 1970s Derek Prince even established the Shepherding movement with the intent of reigning in the independency of ministries by, unfortunately, submitting to more senior ministers rather than having plural leadership under the authority of the Word. Another voluntary organization that oversees the fellowship of Word of Faith ministries is The International Convention of Faith Ministries (ICFM). And most of the Word of Faith ministers have been very critical of traditional churches as they claim that they now possess new revelation pertaining to church administration and hermeneutics. In fact, disdain towards professional theological training and hierarchical church structure in favour of voluntary association and anti-intellectual hermeneutics can be traced all the way to Hagin and Kenyon.

Yet one of the challenges of lacking accountability is the fact that such makes it is easy for unsound teachings to go unchecked. And since the charismatic leader of a prosperity church is its highest authority, it is noteworthy that his or her scandals directly affect the entire ministry. In view of seeming successes such as numerical growth and media presence, which can entail an increase in financial revenue and popularity, church polity centralized on the leader or founder can easily give birth to myths and legends haloed in the 'touch not the anointed of God' eisegesis. In fact, the extreme dependency of the prosperity gospel devotee to the prosperity gospel preacher, not to God or the Word of God, is very disturbing and gives ample room for exploitation. Bear in mind that virtually all prosperity preaching churches have one sole leader compared to the traditional church structure where a leader is a part of and answerable to a board. Whereas pride or misinformation screams for independence, Scripture presents a church that is structured and has leadership accountability. Controversies are not far from a minister who lacks accountability. And a wayward minister does not only bring shame upon himself but disrepute to the Body of Christ as well. The personality cult that characterizes the prosperity movement goes hand in glove with the end-times phenomenon which the Apostle Paul forewarned about: "But know this, that in the last days perilous times will come: For men will be lovers of themselves, boasters, proud, blasphemers ... lovers of pleasure rather than lovers of God, having a form of godliness but denying its power. And from such people turn away!"[41]

A minister who lacks accountability indeed opens himself to vulnerability. Hence it is not a wonder that some prosperity preachers constantly find themselves in controversies that have nothing to do with the glory of God – controversies that stem from pride, expressed in selfishness. Dr Craig Blomberg again points out: "But both sexual immorality and material selfishness stem from the same self-indulgent attitudes, and it is little wonder that the two increasingly appear together in our affluent Western world as well."[42]

Got Questions Ministries gives quite a detailed outline on some common traits of prosperity preachers: "The core of his/her messages is always God's desire to bless everyone; There is little, if any, mention of Jesus' words about self-denial, taking up our crosses, or dying to the flesh (Luke 9:23; Matthew 10:38, 16:24); Almost all their teaching focuses on the gratification of fleshly desires rather than spiritual transformation (Romans 8:29); Obedience to God's commands is rarely mentioned as a prerequisite to His blessing (Jeremiah 18:10); Positive thinking about oneself and one's situation is often equated with faith and is presented as the means by which one can obtain financial blessing; There is a marked absence of any teaching on the necessity of suffering in the life of a believer (2 Timothy 2:12; 3:12; Romans 8:17; Philippians 1:29); Very little distinction is made between God's children and the unsaved in the positive promises of the message (Malachi 3:16–18; Romans 9:15–16); The speaker rarely attempts any type of real Bible teaching that does not support the continual message of positivity and blessing (1 Corinthians 3:1–3); He or she stays away from passages that contradict the positive spin of the message (2 Timothy 4:3); Personal wealth of the minister is often far above the average lifestyle of his congregation (Psalm 49:16–17); The only attributes of God ever mentioned are love and generosity. Scant attention is given to His holiness, justice, and righteousness (Ephesians 4:22–23); Neither the wrath of God against sin nor the coming judgment is ever mentioned (Romans 2:5; 1 Peter 4:5); The only 'sins' discussed at length are negativity, poverty, or a person's failure to believe in themselves (1 Corinthians 6:9–10; Philippians 3:3); Forgiveness is emphasized but with very little explanation of the repentance that was so important to Jesus and the disciples (Matthew 4:17; Mark 6:12; Acts 2:38); The prayer of faith is often referred to as the means by which humans 'leave God no choice but to bless me' (Job 40:1–2)."[43]

The titles of the prosperity preachers' books are explicit enough of the materialistic and anthropocentric themes even without delving into the contents: Joel Osteen's *Your Best Life Now – 7 Steps to Living at Your Full Potential*; Creflo A. Dollar's *Total Life Prosperity: 14*

Practical Steps to Receiving God's Full Blessing; Charles and Annette Capps' *God's Creative Power for Finances*; Shawn Bolz's *Keys to Heaven's Economy: An Angelic Visitation from the Minister of Finance*; John Avanzini's *The Wealth of the World: The Proven Wealth Transfer System*; A. A. Allen's *God's Guarantee to Bless and Prosper You Financially*; Jerry Savelle's *The God of the Breakthrough Will Visit Your House*; Rex Humbard's *Your Key to God's Bank*; Scot Anderson's *Heart of a Billionaire*; Brian Houston's *You Need More Money*; Noel Jones and Scott Chaplan's *Vow of Prosperity: Spiritual Solutions for Financial Freedom* as well as Bruce Wilkinson's *The Prayer of Jabez – Breaking Through to the Blessed Life*. You must question your faith if your Christian bestseller, when read by non-Christians, is loved but it neither causes one to see the need for the Saviour nor be dismayed by the offence of the Cross.

THE AMERICAN DREAM

What other places could be more suitable to birth and flourish the prosperity gospel than the 'land of the free and the home of the brave' whose enshrined dream is to pursue wealth and happiness? The consumer culture of America, as evinced even by its seductive commercials, is a mass-market of positive psychology that turns the mind into a playground. In the secular world, positivism is led by the likes of Oprah Winfrey and Deepak Chopra. The secularization of religion has blurred the line to such an extent that Oprah Winfrey can even interchange pastors with self-help gurus on her show *SuperSoul Sunday* on the Oprah Winfrey Network (OWN). Indeed, when the American Dream charismatically came to church it found an eager and carnal audience. To understand how the American Dream has become central to some churches in America one just needs to watch scripted 'reality' TV programmes of celebrity pastors like *Preachers of L.A.* or *Preachers of Atlanta*. Pastor and theology professor Gordon Fee remarked:"Indeed, the theology of this new 'gospel' seems far more to fit the American dream than it does the teaching of Him who had 'nowhere to lay His head.'[44]

Megachurch scholars Scott Thumma and Dave Travis wrote, "With a combined annual income of seven billion dollars and vast electronic audiences, American megachurches rivalled seminaries, denominations, and religious publishers as a major influence in American religious life."[45]Professor of religion at Duke Divinity School in Durham, North Carolina, Kate Bowler pointed out that the Baptist minister and lawyer, Russell H. Conwell (1843–1925), became a prophet of this gospel of wealth with his famous sermon 'Acres of Diamonds'.[46]

The vast wealth of some celebrity preachers is startling even to secular Mammonites! High-roller lifestyles of sprawling mansions, private jets, television channels, mansions, gold-plated bathroom fixtures, flashy automobiles, multi-million-dollar church buildings, and *air-conditioned doghouses*! For instance, Senator Grassley once remarked about Joyce Meyer: "Just think of a $23,000 marble commode. A lot of money going down the toilet you could say."[47] Although the Joyce Meyer Ministry's explanation that 'commode' referred to a chest of drawers was justifiable, the extravagance was not. Do you know how many starving people can be fed by $23,000 in the Third World? The wealth a pastor has accumulated is now his sermon from the pulpit! "...such an Americanized perversion of the Gospel tends to reinforce a way of life and an economic system that repeatedly oppresses the poor — the very thing that the prophetic message denounces so forcefully. Seeking more prosperity in an already affluent society means to support all the political and economic programs that have made such prosperity available—but almost always at the expense of economically deprived individuals and nations."[48] Yet money-making schemes in the church can arguably not be explained better than in the life of the founder of Scientology, L. Ron Hubbard. The financial policy of Scientology, according to Hubbard, is "make money, make more money, make others to produce so as to make money!"[49] Whereas Scientology would want to be presented as Christian, its multi-millionaire founder and science fiction author denies the existence of God, Heaven or Hell and the deity of Christ and rather teaches his pseudoscience called Dianetics.

Money changers in Jerusalem saw no problem in setting up their booths in the Temple's Court of Gentiles and charging foreigners exorbitant exchange rates – the self-same aliens whose place of worship they had turned into a marketplace! The fact that foreigners needed local currency for the Temple tax and for purchasing animals to sacrifice meant nothing to the church merchants. The inexcusable excuse given, and indeed made to sound religious, was that setting up those stalls in the Temple was a convenient way of fundraising for Temple upkeep. When the Lord arrived, He could discern that the greedy church merchants were not valuing worship but commercializing gold over worshipping God. Hence on two separate occasions, He overturned the moneychanger's tables and drove out the church merchants.[50] In lieu of repenting of this sacrilegious behaviour, the church merchants were indignant and questioned His authority because to them a den of thieves was financially more profitable than a house of worship! Yet tables selling books and DVDs are still being displayed *during* church services today and begging for donations still dominates what is supposedly Christian TV programming.

African American Christian communities were easily drawn towards this Wall Street gospel because of its promise to bridge the inequalities gap, even if the promises came heavily tagged along with magic practices like voodoo, visualization, and channelling. And this malevolent concoction of the materialistic American Dream and African occultism has had a terrible socio-economic impact, particularly in the Third World. In view of the background of systematic discriminatory methods that were designed to impoverish African Americans, such as slavery, preaching focused on the accumulation of material wealth was more than welcome compared to the traditional churches' sermons which were considered too spiritual and too focused on Heaven rather than addressing issues on Earth. Eric Lincoln and Lawrence Mamiya wrote: "It is clearly evident that black churches had a major role in establishing the black self-help tradition during a time when there were no social welfare agencies and private philanthropy was reserved for other groups. The Black Church assumed the task of helping black people internalize the ethic of economic rationality that would lead to economic mobility. Black church leaders were well aware of the role of racism in retarding this mobility, and they knew from experience that they and their children would have to put forth maximum efforts for minimal achievements. To reduce the trauma of these realities as much as possible, the black churches took on economic roles and functions and created institutional vehicles they might otherwise have left to other entities."[51] Dr Frederick Eikerenkoetter II would encourage his followers to enjoy the good life here and now rather than wait for 'the pie in the sky' when they die.

Flamboyant leaders like Dr Frederick J. Eikerenkoetter II, popularly known as Reverend Ike, who changed the verse "the love of money is the root of all evil" to the 'lack' of money is the root of all evil, George Baker popularly known as 'Father Divine' and Charles Manuel Grace nicknamed 'Sweet Daddy Grace' were instrumental in bringing the prosperity gospel to the African American communities. Johnnie Colemon popularly regarded as the First Lady of New Thought and her predecessor and founder of Antioch Association of Metaphysical Science Dr H. Lewis Johnson are usually the forgotten figures that were also instrumental in the formation of prosperity gospel in the African American community. "Colemon founded the first predominantly Black Unity congregation. New Thought metaphysical teachings, synthesized with charismatic Christianity, are the ideological basis for today's Word of Faith movement. Thus, Colemon should be thought of as a forerunner of the contemporary African American Faith teachers, although she is not generally thought of this way. Colemon's gender should not be overlooked. There are not many prominent African American women out front in the Word of Faith Movement. For the most part, the women who are visible generally play a secondary role as part of a ministry team headed by their husbands. It is likely, that Colemon is not as well recognized as Fred Price or others of today's male Faith teachers, because she was a church founder and pastor at a time when it was not generally acceptable for women to hold that office."[52] In view of their materialistic theologies which were mixed with New Thought metaphysics, these African American charismatic leaders cannot just be viewed as forerunners of the prosperity gospel in the African American communities but as equally instrumental in the formation of the Word of Faith movement itself.

In no particular order, the prominent prosperity preachers, who are all virtually from America, include Kenneth and Lynette Hagin, Kenneth and Gloria Copeland, Granville 'Oral' Roberts and his son Richard, T. L. Osborn, A. A. Allen, John Osteen, Joel and Victoria Osteen, Joyce Meyer, Pat Robertson, Morris Cerullo, Charles Capps, Kathryn Kuhlman and her protégé Benny Hinn, Jesse Duplantis, Paula White, Lester Sumrall, Norvel Hayes, Robert Tilton, Jerry Savelle, Roy Hicks, John Praise, Casey and Wendy Treat, Jan and Paul Crouch, Todd Bentley, Charles Cowan, Rex Humbard, Marilyn and Wally Hickey, Billy Joe Daugherty, Don Gossett, Francis and Charles Hunter, Bob Jackson, Charles Ellis III and Charles and Myrtle Fillmore, founders of the influential New Thought movement called Unity School of Christianity. Prominent African American prosperity preachers include Creflo Dollar who, interestingly, even wrote the book *Unmasking the Spirit of Mammon*, Eddie Long, Ira V. Hilliard, Carlton Pearson, Frederick K.C. Price, considered the godfather of Prosperity Gospel in African American churches, the modalist T.D. Jakes, who writes mostly on emotional healing, as well as Leroy Thompson of the prosperity books *Money Cometh! To the Body of Christ* and *I'll Never Be Broke Another Day in My Life*. The prominence of the South American John Avanzini and the South Korean David Yongi Cho in this Rolls-Royce gospel should also be noted.

On the other hand, Christian ministers and writers who have stood up, and some still continue to stand, against this so-called prosperity gospel include David Jones, J. C. Ryle, Paul Washer, Russell Woodbridge, Bill Muehlenberg, Karen Bullock, Conrad Mbewe, Stuart Mackay, Lisa Withrow, Dan R. McConnell, Jerry Falwell, Richard Bargas, Warren W. Wiersbe, John Perkins, R. Albert Mohler, Ben Witherington III, John MacArthur, John Piper, Ron Kubsch, Bob Johnson, DeForest B. Soaries Jr, Judith Hill, Gordon Fee, Jonathan Leeman, Mark Dever, Wayne Grudem, Craig Blomberg, Steven J. Lawson, Charles Farah Jr, Lars Wilhelmsson, John Stott, Michael Catt, Summer Jaeger, Miguel Núñez, Michael Otieno Maura, Femi Adeleyi, Costi Hinn, Kenneth Mbugua and even Jim Bakker! Even the Latter-day Saints apostle Dallin Oaks criticized the prosperity movement: referring to the Parable of the Sower, he warned against attitudes that have a fixation on the acquisition, utilization, or possession of the property. He further pointed out that affluent people are in a particular danger of being sedated by materialism.[53] Interestingly, even megachurch celebrity pastor,

Rick Warren, condemns the prosperity gospel for its excessive focus on materialism and the showiness of its flamboyant leadership.

Steven Harris, a PhD student in American Religious History at Harvard University, graduated from Yale, Vanderbilt and Southern Baptist Theological Seminary and also served as assistant pastor for a Kentucky Baptist church, critiqued T.D. Jakes' *Reposition Yourself: Living Life Without Limits* thus: "Dubbed 'America's Best Preacher' by *Time* magazine, T.D. Jakes has become a household name and a revered spiritual authority among many professed Christians and, even recently, among some conservative evangelicals... *Reposition Yourself* consists of fifteen chapters divided into three major sections: 'The Sky's the Limit,' 'Beyond the Limits of Mediocrity,' and 'Beyond the Limits of Success.' These sections could easily be titled, 'Wanting Prosperity,' 'Pursuing Prosperity,' and 'Managing Prosperity,' respectively... While Jakes is prudent enough to avoid flagrant prosperity gospel rhetoric — even warning against the desire for riches at times — he still equates success with things like a closed business deal, a house, and a Mercedes. Moreover, throughout the book, he refers to such figures as Oprah and Sean 'Diddy' Combs as examples of those living the successful life, worthy of imitation."[54]

In 2007, Senator Chuck Grassley of the Senate Finance Committee launched an investigation on six famous prosperity teachers: Joyce Meyer, Benny Hinn, Creflo Dollar, Eddie Long, Kenneth and Gloria Copeland as well as Paula White. Whereas Paula White ministries verbally expressed the willingness to corporate, in 2009 only the ministries of Joyce Meyer and Benny Hinn had been cleared from 'the Grassley Six'. The ministries of Eddie Long, the Copelands, and Creflo Dollar declined to comply with the investigation citing the interference of the state into church matters.[55]

THE PROSPERITY GOSPEL IN AFRICA

Considering the American Dream, it is no wonder that virtually all prominent prosperity preachers emanate from America. Yet while the prosperity gospel indeed emanated from the United States of America, it must be noted that the Third World did not only import but adapted it to suit their local adherents. Hence one of the prominent features of the prosperity gospel in Africa is the so-called prophetic ministry. This comes as no surprise in an impoverished continent vexed by fears of witchcraft and so-called generational curses. Some of the prosperity preachers from the Third World include Nicholas Duncan-Williams, Edir Macedo, Matthew Ashimolowo, Benson Idahosa, Enoch Adeboye, David Oyedepo — without forgetting the prophets who brought prosperity preaching to dizzying heights in my homeland, Zimbabwe: Walter Magaya, Uebert Angel, and Emmanuel Makandiwa.

Referring to the effect of prosperity gospel in Africa, Pastor Conrad Mbewe blogged: "Evidently, this junk originated from mega-churches in the USA and then found ready soil in West Africa, and especially in Nigeria. Having given it an African flavour, it is now being exported across Africa at a phenomenal rate... The *Africanisation* of this religious junk is primarily in the way it has been made to appeal to African spirituality. The pastor is the modern witchdoctor calling all and sundry to come to him for 'deliverance.' Just as the witchdoctor appealed to us by inviting us to see him for spiritual protection or when we were struggling with bad luck, childlessness, joblessness, illness, failure to attract a suitor for marriage or to rise in a job or get a contract, etc., these pastors do precisely the same thing.... Let's face it: this is our African traditional religions coming into the church through the back door."[56]

In Nigeria, there are many prosperity preachers but Benson Idahosa, a young firebrand, became the preacher most identified with this movement. He would go on to arguably become the father of the prosperity gospel in Africa. He earned his place in history, however, not just because he was the first African to articulate the message, but because of how he took this theology to the masses. Idahosa, against the trend in the society of his time, preached that Christians ought to have access to material wealth and live life to the full, insisting that he would no longer drive the two-door Volkswagen Beetle car that was in vogue and mostly used by the average wage earner but only ride four-door cars such as the Mercedes Benz and the Peugeot of the bourgeoisies. He also insisted that members of his church should not tithe nor give offerings with coins, but currency notes of high worth.[57]

South Africa has not been spared by the prosperity gospel either as the Commission for the Promotion and Protection of the Rights of Cultural, Religious and Linguistic Communities (CRL Rights Commission) now has its hands full particularly from the controversies of the movement! The world has repeatedly been shocked by unconventional, or unscriptural rather, methods employed in some prophetic ministries where adherents are commanded to do unspeakable things: while one prophet in South Africa sprayed his followers with the insecticide Doom and claimed that it heals and casts out demons, another had a video on his Facebook page where he was feeding dog meat to his followers with this caption, 'It is not what goes through the mouth that disqualifies us and defile us but what comes out of the mouth – the heart matters most than what decomposes (the food we eat).' According to eNCA he also claimed to have turned his church members into snakes in 2016 and also asked them to get naked before praying *to* him. As if such scandals were not enough, yet another gave his congregates rat poison mixed with water in order to prove that death had no power over believers! Still another instructed his adherents to go outdoors and graze like cattle and … they obeyed him! Realizing that South Africa is a secular state with full guarantees of freedom of religion, thereby the state cannot control the church, the Commission has now approached the parliament to amend the act on regulation, or self-regulation, of, in this case, churches.

Some of the Christian leaders in the First World that I interact with admit that they do not have an in-depth understanding of the prosperity gospel and Word of Faith narrative within the African context. The book *"Church Mafia: Captured by Secret Powers"* is a true story of Makhado Ramabulana. The bible student who became an ordained pastor left orthodox Christianity and became a 'prophet' in the occult in order to build a megachurch and deceive a multitude of followers with staged miracles, demonic powers as well as the commercialization of the Gospel. The accounts are spine-chilling but the repentance is humbling.

3.   PROSPERITY THEOLOGY

When one critiques the prosperity gospel, the expectation is that one should just name and shame those who are ostensibly greedy. But that is not solely the case because misplaced preaching about money is essentially a by-product of the Word of Faith theology. In other words, the prosperity gospel can be fully understood by exposing the faulty theological underpinnings upon which it rests. Hence some of the leaders may not necessarily be known for preaching material wealth, but their folk theology is still Word of Faith dogmatics. Some prosperity gospel preachers even avoid money matters that may come across as controversial in the public eye yet they share the same theology with the ostensible money-grabbers. In fact, both the ostensible money-grabbers and those who publicly present themselves as not interested in prosperity preaching are all getting money from the heresy; inasmuch as getting a huge following through speaking messages identifying with and patting carnal nature on the shoulders at the expense of the Gospel will still make money from the financial contributions coming from such huge followings. For instance, whereas Joel Osteen claims that he does not preach about money, in March 2014 more than $600,000 was stolen from Lakewood Church and that cash was only from *one weekend's offerings*.

Scholar and Pastor Dan McConnell points out that "any new religious movement [within Protestantism] must bear the scrutiny of two criteria: biblical fidelity and historical orthodoxy. Regrettably, the Positive Confession movement fails on both counts. The historical roots of this movement (which Charles Farah has called 'Faith Formula Theology') lie in the occult, and most recently, in New Thought and its offshoot, the Mind Science cults. Its Biblical basis is found only in the peculiar interpretations of its own leaders, not in generally accepted Christian theology."[58] Indeed, Charles Farah Jr who served as Professor of Theology and Historical Studies at Oral Roberts University, clearly expresses that Word of Faith movement's teachings are more presumptive than genuine. He asserts that "from Kenyon comes a specific strand of religious humanism that is developed by the word of faith theology. It has been developed into a form of charismatic humanism. The result is a disproportionate emphasis on the present world, where revelation knowledge becomes the new hermeneutical principle."[59]

THEOLOGICAL EDUCATION

Prosperity megachurch pastors, with few exceptions, usually possess less formal education than their mainline and evangelical counterparts. Bible schooling within the Word of Faith movement, if any, is essentially in-house as the obedient followers are indoctrinated into the dogmatized viewpoints of the leader. At times, these denominationally equipped students are given certificates and degrees not even worth the paper they are written on since some come from unaccredited schools. After all, the hallmark of the prosperity movement is charisma, not sound theology. Pastors instead bore their ministries on their backs by such mountebankery. Numerous times I have been approached by students with modules that are so watered down that they are not even fit for an adult Sunday school elementary class. Instead of tutoring them, I had to refer them to accredited seminaries with sound theology.

In writing about the prosperity heresy, Pastor Lars Wilhelmsson explains how anti-intellectualism is one of the characteristics of cults: "Anti-Intellectualism: This does not mean that cult leaders or followers are not intelligent; it means that they have a general disdain for education as offered by our society and religious institutions. The cultist takes pride in his lack of formal education, often making fun of seminaries by referring to them as 'cemeteries.' Cult leaders are for the most part 'self-taught,' deciding for themselves what is important and what is not important to study. If they do have some formal or semiformal education, it is often at a school that is not accredited by an accrediting association. Such a lack of formal education without the willingness to be subject to the judgment of others easily leads to heresy since a person is not given the broad spectrum of education, whether secular or theological. I'm reminded of the young and enthusiastic evangelist who told John Wesley, 'God doesn't need your education.' Wesley responded, 'Nor does God need your ignorance.' Wesley understood that to bypass the accumulated knowledge and wisdom of people throughout the ages by selecting a narrow path, if a path at all, of intellectual pursuit, is the height of intellectual and religious snobbery."[60]

EISEGESIS

Whereas exegesis is the exposition of Scripture by the objective analysis of a passage with respect to its grammar, syntax and setting, its opposite, eisegesis, is the subjective interpretation of a text which fundamentally means one is trying to give validity to one's presupposed opinion by quoting Scripture. The prosperity gospel can only be exalted at the expense of Scriptural hermeneutics. In fact, the proliferation of this poisonous doctrine has thrived on most of the Christians' lack of knowledge. To assert that most Christians lack sound knowledge of the Bible may seem misplaced particularly in view of the fact that technology has globalized the world into a small village where information is just a fingertip away. Yet that is the very crux of the matter: the information being disseminated on most Christian media outlets is predominantly Word of Faith! And the fact that sound theology is openly scoffed at by Word of Faith leaders explains why the masses continue to be fed this opium of heretics. Prosperity theology leads to doctrinal and material poverty inasmuch as numerical church growth does not correspond to spiritual wellbeing.

The eisegesis of Scripture texts that are meant to evince the prosperity heresy by preachers, pastors and prophets of wealth is appalling. Eisegesis is applied in texts such as Genesis 12:1-3, Deuteronomy 16:16, Jeremiah 29:11, Matthew 25:14-30, Luke 6:38, John 10:10, 19:23-24, Acts 19:11-12, Philippians 4:13, Galatians 3:14, II Corinthians 8:9, and III John 2. For instance, the term used for 'prosper' in III John 2 has nothing to do with material wealth at all inasmuch as the text is simply a generic salutation of Apostle John to Elder Gaius! Referring to III John 2, Robin Brace of the ministry UK Apologetics comments: "Prosperity teachers claim the word is all about prosperity which reveals their lack of knowledge of New Testament Greek. The claim which one sometimes hears is that 'prosper' at the beginning of this verse concerns prosperity of a financial nature while 'prospers' at the conclusion of the verse only concerns spiritual matters. But this is entirely incorrect and - in both cases - the same Greek word is being used (eudow). Indeed, if John the Apostle expresses his wish that the elder might prosper 'in all things' does not this remark itself shows that this is not being confined to one's financial life?"[61]

Whereas the term 'poor' in Luke 4:18 is spiritual and refers to those in need of the Good News, it is not surprising that prosperity preacher Rod Parsley chose to interpret the text with the Word of Faith eisegesis: "For you to sit in physical bondage is to deny the power of the gospel. Most people would have no trouble shouting whatsoever if I said, 'To remain in the bondage of sin and death is to deny the power of the gospel.' If I said the same thing about poverty and financial bondage, it would get as quiet as a tomb. If I said that for you to live from paycheck to paycheck is to deny the power of the gospel, many of you would get angry. In Luke 4:18, notice there was an anointing to preach good news to the poor. A lot of people do not like to look at that because the good news to a poor man is that he doesn't have to be poor anymore. We have multitudes saved, delivered, and filled with the Holy Ghost, and many are healed, yet over 90% of the church of Jesus Christ are living in absolute financial bondage. All the while, Jesus is saying, 'I've been anointed to preach the good news to the poor.' You have held back the flow. You have denied the perpetual propulsion of power that could deliver you from not only sin and sickness but from the horrible stench of poverty."[62]

The prosperity heresy can only be established by proof-texting because it is impossible to defend the Prosperity Movement with either contextual or topical hermeneutics. Professor Judith L. Hill, who has served as a missionary and lived and taught in Ethiopia, Nigeria and now Central African Republic, where she is a head of the department of New Testament and Greek, wrote: "It is important to note that those who follow the Prosperity Gospel are often rather weak or unconcerned regarding the rules of hermeneutics and their use of the insights of Greek and Hebrew syntax. These insufficiencies lead to inadequate interpretations of passages and even taking passages out of their linguistic and historical contexts."[63]

As earlier noted, the very fact that Word of Faith leaders have a very low view, if any, of professional theological training, reflects in the Word of Faith adherents as well inasmuch as mere memorization of Scripture and piecemeal interpretation thereof are lauded at the expense of the topical and contextual exegesis. It is very disappointing to listen to the eisegesis of a church leader who thinks cherry-picking and quoting Scripture is tantamount to ministering the Word. To make matters worse, such leaders have the liberty to go and write Bible commentaries! It is not exegesis to try to sound fancy by attempting to explain a Greek term in a verse without giving heed to the contextual and topical understanding of the subject. If the leader has such a faulty understanding of Scripture, what more the adherents feeding from the pasture of this eisegesis? No wonder prosperity gospel adherents are taught that 'praying the Word' is quoting Scripture verse after verse in your prayers and anything contrary to the favour of God upon your life must be bound by quoting Bible verses. Making a presentation at the Zimbabwe Open University's 2013 Vice Chancellor's Day, which was also submitted for publication in the International Open and Distance Learning Journal, Dr David Bishau aptly remarked: "Our basic misgiving with the dogmatic approach is that we will have as many meanings of the text as we have interpreters of the Bible if people are at liberty to read into the text their own meanings that ignore the author's meaning and intent. What we see with prosperity gospel preachers are already established dogmatic positions that are then supported by biblical texts that originally had nothing to do with the dogmas being propelled by the preachers. They stand way apart from authorial intent. So, basically what the prosperity gospel preachers are doing is to snatch verses from the Bible and run with them, but not only do they run with them they also run with them to the sea and dive!"[64]

MODERN-DAY GNOSTICISM

Pauline epistles, particularly one written to the church at Colosse, essentially countered the seductive syncretism of Gnostics which was influential in the New Testament era and became a challenge to the early church. The dangerous heresy, which became more prominent in the second century, was designed to sound like "well-crafted arguments."[65] The writings upon which Gnosticism was based were fraudulent forgeries which have recently been shamefully presented as 'lost books of the Bible'. The Word of God is inerrant in its trustworthiness, sufficient for believers to understand salvation and harmonious in its diversity hence any attempt to reconcile any of the so-called lost books to the Bible is futile and impossible because any of these forgeries are an epic contradiction to the Bible. Gnosticism disregarded sin, presented a novel Jesus who was more magical than historical and even went further on to claim that Christ was not the exclusive way to God.

Indeed the underpinning theology of the Word of Faith movement is the so-called revelation knowledge. If there is a fault in this revelation knowledge, then it goes without saying that every other tenet of this belief is faulty as well. General revelation, at times referred to as Natural Theology, evinces the self-existence and supremacy of God over His creation through the intelligent and natural order of creation. Special revelation is the unique method God miraculously revealed Himself and, through the inspiration of the Holy Spirit, gave the doctrines of faith. Since Scripture and Christian theology only recognize general revelation and special revelation, the so-called revelation knowledge is Gnostic in nature inasmuch as it makes extra-biblical and counter-biblical claims. Inasmuch as God evinced His truthfulness and faithfulness through the harmony of Scripture from the Book of Genesis to the Book of Revelation, it is beyond question that any teaching, new or old, which contradicts the Word must be rejected. Word of Faith ministers actually thrive on telling their adherents the new revelation they got from presumed dialogues with God. The frequency of their so-called conversations with God is so unnerving that even the inspired writers of the Bible never had such a privilege. Yet what is most disturbing is the fact that this new unverifiable revelation is the standard of faith in the Word of Faith movement to such an extent that even the authority of Scripture is overruled. The level of trust the Word of Faith ministers require from their followers is unheard of: they have a special word from the Lord which cannot be found anywhere else, not even in the Bible, so everyone simply has to trust them! Ironically, if their claims are verified with Scripture, they are consistently found to be false. If the Word of Faith movement had hierarchical structures to verify ministers according to Scriptural orthodoxy and thereby hold the self-same ministers to account, virtually all of them would have been defrocked.

Prosperity theology is inherently Gnostic in nature inasmuch as what is deemed revelation is nothing less than extra-biblicism which is claimed to be given directly by the spirit to the man of God, who also enjoys angelic visitations even from some whose names are withheld in the Bible but only revealed to him. (There is no need to capitalize the term 'spirit' because God does not contradict Himself.) The so-called revelation cannot be questioned because it is alleged that questioning the man of God is tantamount to questioning God who called and anointed His servant. The claim by prosperity preachers to have special revelation into the mysteries of God is terribly uncanny, yet what is uncannier are the striking similarities between the prosperity heresies and dogmas of the New Age. Secret societies claim to have esoteric and exoteric knowledge. Exoteric knowledge is what is fed to the public and esoteric knowledge is only reserved for the select few. Whereas the Bible is clear that all the mysteries of God sufficient for our salvation are revealed in Scripture,[66] prosperity heretics claim that God reveals some things that are only for them to know and for the congregates to obey. Any form of prophecy which claims to supersede Scripture should gladly be trampled upon.

This Gnostic version of presenting novel Christianity is very worrying inasmuch as the preacher is, in the process, claiming to have special knowledge or understanding that is not available to the rest of the Christians. The uniqueness of the revelation is heightened by claims of unheard of 'visions' that cannot be exegetically confirmed by Scripture. And, as aforementioned, to question the revelation is to have a rebellious spirit because the congregation should 'touch not the anointed of God.' Yet while we Protestants unequivocally scoff at Rome's dogma of papal infallibility, the untouchable and unquestionable nature of these prosperity leaders is also tantamount to papal infallibility. Having revelations that can neither be questioned nor verified becomes the bedrock of all sorts of delusions. If the leader realizes error in his interpretation, he does not state that he was in error but would rather say he had not yet received the 'full revelation' – even in cases where the prior 'revelation' and the new 'revelation' are not a progression but a contradistinction! Whereas doctrinal reliability of the Word of Faith churches is hampered by newer revelations always championed as the best there is, most traditional churches, which they castigate, maintain orthodoxy by passing on the same old doctrines from generation to generation. Scripture is consistent in maintaining that the intent of a false minister is always personal gain.

Considering the orthodox and historic tenets of evangelicalism, it is an impropriety which borders on a joke in very bad taste to denote Word of Faith ministers' evangelicals. Indeed, the movement is a neo-Pentecostal contemporary subculture that fundamentally has liberals, Charismatics, and Pentecostals of all stripes basking under its sun. Evangelicals who walk into the movement are in essence taking on a new identity called neo-evangelicalism inasmuch as one cannot uphold extra-biblical and counter-biblical heresies and still claim to be affirming the inerrancy and sufficiency of Scripture. That is a paradox of epic proportions. The argument that this prosperity heresy can be classified as quasi-cult because it mixes truth with errors fails to see that deception and the prideful worship of Mammon can be both cultic and occultly.

At the heart of the so-called positive confession of the prosperity movement is the uncanny belief that believers are little gods. Therefore, just as God spoke things into existence at Creation, so His children can also speak whatever they desire into life. Word of Faith proponents blatantly claim that the creation of Adam was God's desire to recreate Himself therefore we are little gods just as Adam was a deity. Adam is not just claimed to be man-god. He is claimed to have had the fullness of the Godhead within him! On what basis then can creation be equal to the Creator? Nowhere in Scripture does stewardship translate to ownership. God never gave the world either to Adam or to Satan! This pantheistic heresy nicknamed 'name it and claim it' resonates with the lure of the Serpent in the Garden that Adam and Eve would be just like God if they ate from the forbidden tree.[67] Regardless of the interpretation one gives to the creation account of man, the fact clearly remains that God self-exists and man is His creation. After being coached that you possess what you confess, positive confession then becomes the faith formula of the prosperity doctrine. Morris Cerullo said, "Did you know that from the beginning of time the whole purpose of God was to reproduce Himself? ... who are you? Come on, say it: 'Sons of God'! Come on, say it! And what does work inside us, brother, is that manifestation of the expression of all that God is and all that God has. And when we stand up here, brother, you are not looking at Morris Cerullo; you're looking at God. You're looking at Jesus."[68] Such claims may as well be classified as the papal infallibility version of prosperity preachers. It truly comes as no surprise that a person who considers himself to be 'God' would write an autobiography titled *The Legend of Morris Cerullo*. And who else could give the front cover commendation of the book other than Joel Osteen!

True to nature, prosperity theologians have made some declarations that are shockingly blasphemous to the extent one winces in trying to think that such utterances are made by Christians, let alone ministers! Author and scholar Hank Hanegraaff succinctly rebutted the deification of man by summarizing Word-Faith pantheism thus: "God created man in 'God's class', as 'little gods', with the potential to exercise what they refer to as the 'God kind of faith' in calling things into existence and living in prosperity and success as sovereign beings. Of course, we forfeited this opportunity by rebelling against God in the Garden and taking upon ourselves Satan's nature. To correct this situation, Jesus Christ became a man, died spiritually (thus taking upon Himself Satan's nature), went to Hell, was 'born again', rose from the dead with God's nature again, and then sent the Holy Spirit so that the incarnation could be duplicated in believers, thus fulfilling their calling to be what they call 'little gods'. Since we are called to experience this kind of life now, we should be successful in virtually every area of our lives. To be in debt, then, or be sick, or (as is even taught by the faith teachers) to be left by one's spouse, simply means you don't have enough faith – or you have some secret sin in your life, because if you didn't, you would be able to handle all these problems."[69] Little gods? Jesus taking upon Himself Satan's nature! Jesus born again? Incarnation duplicated in believers? That sounds more New Age than Christology!

Yet it is the granddaddies of the movement, Hagin and Copeland, who are prominent in this blasphemous theology insomuch that we are taught over and over that Jesus actually became Satan on the Cross and went to Hell! Using the so-called revelation knowledge to explain I Timothy 3:16, Copeland claimed that the fact God justified Jesus means Jesus was not righteous. He claimed that Jesus became sin hence the Father forsook Him at Calvary and He went to hell on behalf of believers: "Why do you think Moses, obeying the instruction of God, hung the serpent upon the pole instead of a lamb? That used to bug me. I said, 'Why in the world would you want to put a snake up there — the sign of Satan? Why didn't you put a lamb on that pole?' And the Lord said, 'Because, it was the sign of Satan that was hanging on the cross.'"[70] Jesus had to be justified, because He was unrighteous? Jesus accepted the sin nature of Satan? Jesus was the sign of Satan hanging on the Cross? Who are these men! Viewing the Prosperity Movement as just another contemporary phenomenon within the Church misses the point altogether. The Prosperity Movement is a demonic enterprise that must be classified as blasphemous.

POSITIVISM

Positive confession has a very low view, if any, of the sovereignty of God inasmuch as this so-called law of attraction reduces God to something subservient to these confessions. In essence, man has ascended to a position of deity and God has been reduced to be a man's servant who is ever ready to do man's bidding. In fact, man's words are considered so powerful that, if spoken negatively, can thwart God's sovereign plans on our lives. Celebrity pastor Joel Osteen said, "Why did God take away his speech? It is because God knew that Zachariah's negative words would cancel out His plans ... See, God knows the power of our words. He knows that we prophesy our future ... And He knew that Zachariah's own negative words would stop His plan."[21] To be God, or little gods as the Word of Faith heretical theology claims, has always been Satan's main agenda.[72]

Gaslighted followers are instructed to 'claim their blessings' because it is their 'season, destiny, appointed time, divine appointment ... of breakthroughs to abundant, floodgates of finances.' This 'word of faith' theology, which alleges that one should curse Satan then just name the blessing one wants in order to claim it is a leaf probably from the pages of Mesmer rather than Scripture. In fact, prosperity preachers claim that if one declares something and believes it, God is put in a corner and, therefore, has no option but to act upon one's declaration! God put in a corner? Which god is this who exists to serve the whims of His creation? Since poverty and sickness are perceived to be curses, a poor or sick person then is alleged to be out of favour with God. Being poor or sick in the Word of Faith movement is in fact seen as a sign of weak faith. Women are being sexually exploited under the guise of cleansing from barrenness by perverts masquerading as men of God.

Eudaemonism is the belief that God intends for us to experience continued, unbroken physical health, financial wealth, and emotional euphoria in this fallen world. Frederick Price, a man who has proclaimed a lot of nonsensical eudaemonism, claimed, "The believer should never die before the age of 70. That is the minimum and then they should live to be 120 years. This is done by faith words. If you keep talking death, that is what you are going to have. If you keep talking sickness and disease, that is what you are going to have, because you are going to create the reality of them with your own mouth. That is a divine law."[73] Christians are neither masters of their destinies nor captains of their ships. God is! Therefore, whatever utterances believers may declare still mean nothing if they do not abide in the will of God.

J. Kwabena Asamoah-Gyadu, Professor of Contemporary African Christianity and Pentecostal/Charismatic Theology at the Trinity Theological Seminary in Ghana, points out: "The explanations offered for setbacks in terms of 'unconfessed sin', 'non-fulfilment of monetary obligations to God and the church', 'negative confessions' and 'lack of faith' are simply inappropriate and insufficient as far as the enigmas of life are concerned. The result has been the pain, suffering and disappointment caused to many believers through these principles. It is simply unrealistic, pastorally insensitive, and unbiblical to preach that Christians could enjoy a pain-free, problem-free life merely by 'positive confession' and payment of tithes. In the experience of Paul, it is in carrying in one's body the death of Jesus that the life of the resurrected Christ may also be revealed in the body of the believer (II Corinthians 4:9–10)."[74]

Word of Faith is indeed a novel brand of Christianity with a test of positive confession that even our Lord and His apostles would have failed. Come to think of it! Instead of the so-called positive teaching that God loves everyone, the Lord and His apostles would teach that sinful and unrepentant people are going to Hell; instead of the positive teaching that God wants to bless everyone, the Lord and His apostles would maintain that whoever does not submit to the Lordship of Christ is accursed and depraved. Jesus delighted in the will of God, not so-called positive confession: He felt anger and drove moneychangers from the

Temple. He even failed to obey the prosperity preachers' favourite Bible quote of "touch not the anointed of God" by pronouncing woes on the religious leaders of His day and even calling them "hypocrites", "blind guides" and "whitewashed tombs". The apostles would call some teachers and apostles and prophets false. And the Apostle Paul would go on to charge that those who thought that they can be saved by circumcision may as well go further and castrate themselves! Surely the Lord and His apostles would dismally fail this amazing version of positive confession Christianity.

The disturbing reasoning of the prosperity theology is that at Creation God gave man dominion on Earth to live a life not lacking anything. It claims that man had so much dominion that even if He, God, wanted to involve Himself in the affairs of Earth He had to consult man first! Then at the Fall man forfeited dominion and Satan now had power over the Earth, including the power that man once had. So even God had no access to His creation hence He came with the plan of bringing Jesus in the form of man to give Satan a knockout blow and take back the power! It is not necessarily the blatant heresy in this theology that boggles the mind but the equal level of arrogance and conviction by which it is carried out. It is carried out with a conviction that rules out ignorance. This is an expertly devised scheme of Satan tailor-made to mislead and deceive naive congregates by displaying lucrative but illusive promises that identify with the carnal nature.

The very fact that the movement is called Word of Faith means faith is an essential and distinct element of their worldview. Yet, contrary to their teachings, faith is neither positive mental attitude nor just an active force. God, not self, is the object of faith. To place self as the object of faith is not only metaphysical but cultish in nature. It may as well be secular humanism repackaged under the garb of religion. Hence self-help paperbacks fly off the shelves nowadays more than theology books of sound doctrine. David Jones emphasizes, "According to prosperity theology, faith is not a theocentric act of the will, or simply trust in God; rather it is an anthropocentric spiritual force, directed at God. Indeed, any theology that views faith solely as a means of materialistic gain, rather than the acceptance of heavenly justification, must be judged as faulty and inadequate."[75]

ANTHROPOCENTRISM

Rather than being a message of self-denial,[76] the prosperity gospel is a religion of self-satisfaction, self-esteem and self-glorification which thrives in the self-help mass market. By asserting that a believer's mind is a battlefield, Word of Faith's New Thought influence comes full circle and substitutes the Gospel with the 'gospel' of self. Scripture is now replaced with psychology and psychiatry as the prosperity celebrity preachers become therapists diagnosing the mind suffering from inferiority complex and negative confessions.

Preachers become life coaches and sermons become motivational speeches. Thus Peale's and Schuller's schools of positivism become invigorated in the ministries of Joel Osteen, Paula White, Joyce Meyer, Noel Jones, and such alike.

Reviewing Joel Osteen's book, *Break Out! 5 Keys to Go Beyond Your Barriers and Live an Extraordinary Life,* Bob Johnson, senior pastor of Cornerstone Baptist Church in Roseville, Michigan, critiqued: "For the faithful pastor who does not have an audience the size of a stadium, or the believer who never makes it to CEO, Osteen's message of 'hope' is actually one of condemnation. Either you do not dream enough, or something is wrong with your faith. While his message is popular because you are your own saviour, it simply is not true. Pastor, some of your people may like what he has to say and may feel that he is a nice guy with a positive message in a negative world. The problem is when we accept his horrible theology, our entire understanding of Scripture is warped. Joel probably is America's pastor. Sadly, *Break Out!* pastors' people to be narcissistic, biblically illiterate, and theologically confused. In other words, *Break Out!* tells you to suspend biblical discernment and enjoy your day at Disneyworld."[27]

The last thing you expect to find in a Word of Faith Sunday service is the preaching of the Gospel. There is a world of difference between teaching about Jesus and preaching Christ inasmuch as Jesus *is* the very Gospel! In fact, you expect messages tailor-made to look like lectures hence adherents are required to bring notepads and pens to take notes rather than the transforming exegesis of Scripture declaring the uniqueness, supremacy, and sufficiency of Christ in all matters relating to life. Instead, you hear anthropocentric and psychological messages researched from the internet with titles such as 'Ten Points to Abundant Life' or 'Seven Steps to a Better You' or 'How to Have a Healthy Diet'. If the church ceases to be a gathering of believers being continually transformed by the Gospel, then it becomes a self-help service centre where egomaniacs dish out messages formulated by psychology rather than Scripture. 'Pastorpreneurs' or 'gospelpreneurs' doing church business where the flock is nothing less than a meal ticket!

The liveliness required in the Word of Faith messages demands that there should be 'revelations' that must wow the crowd. Furthermore, the change from Christocentrism to anthropocentrism is confirmed by the politically correct methodology of the seeker movement where there is hardly a difference even between the genre of music played in church and the beats of secular music. In some instances, it is only the lyrics that are changed! Gospel music should distinctly be a musical and doxological expression of Scripture. Yet exulting the Godhead can be placed in the periphery of Praise and Worship segments as positive confessions and expectations of health, wealth, victory and 'double portions' are poured forth and God is merely mentioned as a genie. Then, in some churches, there is the midweek cell group fellowship of smaller gatherings in houses where the Sunday service is revisited. Whereas home fellowship is commendable, this service is in fact an appraisal of the Sunday teaching because a critique is strictly forbidden.

The root of the Word of Faith movement and the 'blab it and grab it' message, or 'prosperity gospel' is not biblical and is in many ways antithetical to the true Gospel message. Indeed, it has more in common with New Age metaphysics than with biblical Christianity. Both the metaphysical cults and the 'name it and claim it' teaching distort the truth and embrace the false teaching that our thoughts control reality. Whether it is the power of positive thinking or the prosperity gospel, the premise is the same — what you think or believe will happen is ultimately what controls what will happen. If you think negative thoughts or are lacking in faith, you will suffer or not get what you want. But on the other hand, if you think positive thoughts or just have 'enough faith' then you can have health, wealth, and happiness now. This false teaching appeals to one of man's most basic instincts, man's sinful nature, which is one reason why it is hugely popular. What profit is it to gain the world yet forfeit your soul? Presbyterian theologian, Joseph Haroutunian (1904-68), said: "Before, religion was God-centred. Before, whatever was not conducive to the glory of God was infinitely evil; now that which is not conducive to the happiness of man is evil, unjust, and impossible to attribute to the Deity. Before, the good of man consisted ultimately in glorifying God; now the glory of God consists in the good of man."[78]

And the Lutheran theologian who was Bishop of Strangnas in the Church of Sweden, Gustaf Emanuel Hilderbrand Aulén warned: "Holiness stands as a sentinel against all eudaemonistic and anthropocentric interpretations of religion. Holiness meets us as unconditional majesty. Every attempt to transform the Christian faith into a religion of satisfaction and enjoyment is thereby doomed to failure. Egocentricity masquerading in the robes of religion is excluded. Faith in God cannot be measured and evaluated from the point of view of human happiness and needs, even if these concepts be even so refined and 'spiritualized.' God is not someone faith employs with an eye to the higher or lower advantages which he may be able to furnish; nor is he someone we can call upon in order that our needs and desires may be met. Even if anthropocentricity should disguise itself in the cleverest costume, it will inevitably be unmasked by the Holy One. Every tendency to make God serve human interests is irrevocably doomed."[79]

The Soteriology championed by the Word of Faith movement is synergistic. There is always an element of man playing a role in being saved hence adherents are encouraged to 'make a decision to follow Jesus'. Monergism upholds the doctrine of election, which is hardly mentioned in the Word of Faith churches, and it asserts that God chose the elect even before the foundation of the world.[80] To make a decision to follow Jesus surprisingly means that man, in his depraved state, which the Bible calls 'dead in sin', has the decision concerning his salvation. It is unbiblical to claim that human will and divine grace cooperate in one's salvation.

Prosperity theology attacks biblical salvation with its eisegesis of asserting that the Greek term for salvation, for which its adherents usually prefer its Greek term *sozo*, means wholeness in every aspect of life. Indeed salvation is holistic but this eisegetical interpretation, then, is used to claim that a person who is saved should also be physically healthy and financially prosperous. In this respect, prosperity heretics give a blind eye to the fact that in this fallen world, as in Bible times, even some of the saved are materially poor and some are sick, yet at the glorious imminence of the Lord then salvation will be completely holistic. The synergistic Soteriology of the prosperity theology is at its best expressed in a kind of 'God helps those who help themselves'. The warped reasoning is that after being 'spiritually' saved one has some things he has to do 'materially' to find favour with God! Or, to put it bluntly, it is a salvation by works whereby one must keep on giving money in order to find favour with God.

THE ABRAHAMIC COVENANT

Since the bedrock of the prosperity theology is an erroneous interpretation of Scripture, the Abrahamic Covenant is not spared as well. Arguably no one could articulate this covenant heresy more than the Word of Faith's prominent figure and teacher Kenneth Copeland: "After Adam's fall in the Garden, God needed an avenue back into the earth; since man was the key figure in the Fall, man had to be the key figure in the redemption, so God approached a man named Abram. He re-enacted with Abram what Satan had done with Adam. God offered Abram a proposition and Abram bought it."[81] Now God is reduced to a little genie begging the powerful man to be allowed back into the affairs of the world He created! The eisegesis of the Abrahamic Covenant deliberately gives a blind eye to the fact that the covenant was made by God and was solely dependent on the faithfulness of God. "Prosperity teachers claim that the conduit through which believers receive Abraham's blessings is faith. This completely ignores the orthodox understanding that the Abrahamic covenant was an unconditional covenant. That is, the blessings of the Abrahamic covenant were not contingent upon one man's obedience. Therefore, even if the Abrahamic covenant did apply to Christians, all believers would already be experiencing the material blessings regardless of prosperity theology."[82]

A conditional covenant requires that both parties fulfil the set stipulations and failure by either or both parties means the covenant is nullified. An unconditional covenant is established when one party makes and keeps promises and the other is a recipient with no set requirements. God made and kept His promises to Abraham and no stipulations were made to Abraham. There are no clauses in the agreement requiring Abraham to meet certain conditions for the covenant to be enacted. Hence the Abrahamic Covenant is unconditional. There was nothing Abraham did to deserve the Promised Land and it is not even Israel's military prowess and security intelligence that will enable them to inhabit the entire land God promised. It was God who made the promise and it is God who will fulfil His promise in the Millennium.

In the New Testament, the Judaizers wanted Christians to meet their man-made conditions to enjoy the Abrahamic Covenant and the apostles rejected such a notion inasmuch as even Abraham was not justified by circumcision but by faith. Both in the Old and the New Testament, justification by faith is the method God uses to save. The fact that God would promise redemption to a wayward people – even the patriarchs themselves sinned – evinces that the covenant had nothing to do with their works. And the promise of blessing families of the Earth through Abraham referred to spiritual blessings wrought by Christ through the forgiveness of sins for both Gentiles and Jews. The Apostle Paul's argument is clear even to a layman that Abraham was not justified by observing the law but by having faith in God.[83] Ironically, when the context is crystal clear that the blessings being mentioned refer to believers' spiritual blessings in Christ, to advocate for their carnal message of materialism, prosperity preachers wrench texts out of context in order to claim that the material blessings pronounced on Israel now belong to Gentile Christians. Countless trips are made to Israel with the belief that such will share or transfer material blessings from Israel to the Gentiles.

Professor Gordon Fee exposes the prosperity fallacy thus: "God wills the financial prosperity of every one of his children, and therefore for a Christian to be in poverty is to be outside of God's intended will; it is to be living a Satan defeated life. And usually tucked away with this affirmation is a second: Because we are God's children (the King's kids, as some like to put it) we should always go first class - we should always have the biggest and the best, a Cadillac instead of a Volkswagen, because this alone brings glory to God."[84] The issue with the prosperity doctrine is not necessarily that Christians can be materially rich inasmuch as rich Christians in the New Testament actually used their resources for the advancement of the Gospel. The thorny issue is the claim that *every* Christian must be materially rich! This disguised claim has essentially failed inasmuch as the prime beneficiaries of the prosperity gospel are not every Christian but – guess who – the prosperity preachers themselves! Perchance that is the key intent of this indoctrination after all. Furthermore, some of the prosperity adherents are less educated hence the movement is appealing to them. Inasmuch as the corporate world would require a certain level of education to enjoy its wealth, prosperity gospel simply requires 'enough faith' and a mouth that confesses positively. To the disenfranchised, the prosperity gospel promises upward mobility and to the rich, it justifies their social status since being rich is considered a sign of being blessed by God. Here is the grand question: if confessing wealth brings wealth, why can't prosperity preachers stop asking for donations on each one of their televised programmes? Why can't they just confess wealth and get the money they are begging for?

HEALTH, WEALTH AND HAPPINESS

The prosperity gospel has become the preoccupation of some Pentecostal and Charismatic churches because giving is very central in the church service of prosperity preachers. Prosperity preachers teach that God is transferring or redistributing wealth from the sinners to His children. Hence its message is themed on socio-economic transition. The 1961 edition of the Oxford English Dictionary defines materialism as "devotion to material needs or desires to the neglect of spiritual matters, a way of life ... based entirely on material interests." Yet the link between the prosperity gospel and business workshops and seminars is unmistakable. Some of these workshops are blatantly called Billionaires Clubs! Besides the expensive church auditorium, prosperity churches would rather concentrate on building state of the art cafes and even gymnasiums at the expense of the Great Commission. Nowadays prosperity churches hire business and branding experts to maintain their image and appeal to the broad market. Author and Reader in History and American studies, Randall Stephens points out, "To many within the conservative Protestant fold, the prosperity gospel's brazen divine materialism is as much bad taste as it is bad theology. In 2009, a branch of the Lausanne Movement, an organization founded in part by Billy Graham, described the prosperity gospel as 'false and gravely distorting of the Bible.'"[85]

Mentioning sin is also considered a negative confession. Believers are encouraged to confess grace instead. Yet it is impossible to understand and appreciate grace without understanding the state of the depraved from which one is saved. The Bible teaches that "all who desire to live a godly life in Christ Jesus will be persecuted,"[86] but the 'name it and claim it' message is that any suffering we undergo is simply the result of a lack of faith. The Beatitudes counter the claims that material wealth confirms God's stamp of approval inasmuch as the Lord would consider even those persecuted for their faith in Christ to be blessed. Instead of maintaining that one is saved from the system of this world, the prosperity gospel is completely focused on us getting the things the world has to offer.[87]

Contrary to this modern-day version of Pelagianism, people are not inherently good and only prone to making mistakes here and there. We are all born in sin hence we all need the Saviour. Without abiding in the only Saviour, we are incapable of pleasing God. In lieu of the so-called freedom of the human will, we have a natural proclivity to evil. We are inherently bad and dead in our sins. Contrary to the Word of Faith teachings, we are even incapable of 'deciding to receive Jesus'. Only the grace of God can enable us to follow Jesus. Just as the Church Fathers like Augustine exposed and rebuked monk Pelagius and church councils, starting with the Council of Ephesus in AD 431, condemned Pelagianism, so should we also unequivocally rebuke and expose this anthropocentric heresy.

If health and terrestrial wealth is the measure of success in ministry, how do prosperity preachers explain the fact that one of the most fruitful apostles of the Lord, if not the most fruitful, Apostle Paul, had an ailment throughout his ministry. And despite his prayers for the Lord to take away the pain, the Lord repeatedly maintained that the ailment was actually a good humbling lesson for ministry! How do the prosperity preachers explain that one of the Lord's firebrands, Prophet Jeremiah, is considering the weeping prophet not only because of the Book of Lamentations but because his ministry was essentially characterized by pain and suffering? How about the poor man who rested on Abraham's bosom whilst the rich man was in torment? How do they explain the ministries of the heroes and heroines of faith in Hebrews 11:35-40 some of whom were mocked, wandered as destitute, tortured, imprisoned, and killed! How about Moses who left the Mammon of Pharaoh and chose rather to suffer affliction alongside the children of God? How do prosperity preachers explain multitudes of impoverished Christians in the underground church who are being persecuted and martyred for their faith on a daily basis? Is the prosperity theology not mocking brethren under persecution like the Kurdish Christians currently being slaughtered in Iraq?

The theology of prosperity preachers pertaining to health and wellness is nothing short of Job's Comforters' crocodile tears inasmuch as Eliphaz the Temanite, Bildad the Shuhite, and Zophar the Naamathite maintained that sickness was only a result of sin, therefore, confirmed that one was no longer in God's favour.[88] Even God Himself rebuked this bad theology from the trio who thought they were in the know but Job called them 'miserable comforters'.[89] Countless times painful stories are narrated of the sick who are told to ignore the symptoms of the sickness, as that is a sign of lack of faith, and concentrate on positively confessing that they are well. Bear in mind that even one of the early architects of the Word of Faith movement, Phineas Quimby and his patient Mary Baker Eddy, believed that sickness was nothing but the result of wrong thinking. Sicknesses which, with timely medical care,[90] could have been treated degenerate into fatal conditions because of this blind denial in the name of positivism. The Corinthians had a very tough time accepting the Apostle Paul owing to his rather unimpressive physicality which contradicted their perfect health, wealth, and happiness theology. They would rather have any motivational speaker with rhetoric eloquence like Apollos, who still had to be schooled in the Gospel by Priscilla and Aquila, than the pro-Jesus radical. Apollos humbled himself, got grounded in sound doctrine and became a faithful giant of faith. But the Corinthians would rather celebrate false apostles because they were impressive![91]

Think of the Number One *New York Times* bestselling author, Joel Osteen, who has written motivational books with titles such as: *"Break Out! 5 Keys to Go Beyond Your Barriers and Live An Extraordinary Life"*; *"Every Day A Friday – How to Be Happier 7 Days A Week"*; *"I Declare! 31 Promises to Speak Over Your Life"*; *"It's Your Time: Activate Your Faith, Achieve Your Dreams, and Increase in God's Favour"*; as well as *"You Can! You Will: 8 Undeniable Qualities of a Winner"*! Furthermore, consider Victoria Osteen's book title that summarizes her husband's self-gratification philosophy which is antithetical to Christian ethics: *Love Your Life! Living Happy, Healthy, and Whole*. Joel is a sophist whose messages are more motivational than theological. He told an audience at 'A Night of Hope', Greensboro Convention Centre: "We love you guys. I have just been telling our congregation back home and I am going to declare it over you that 2008 is going to be your best year so far. Well, Joel, what does that mean? You are just up there saying that. It does not mean anything unless you take it in to your heart. This is a *seed* God's trying to deposit on the inside! Why don't you let God birth some new dreams tonight? Why don't you enlarge your vision? … It's going to be a year of promotion, a year of increase, a year of favour, a year of supernatural opportunities!"[92] Interestingly, when Osteen was criticized for being nothing but a motivational speaker, his worship leader at Lakewood Church and Grammy Awards winner Israel Houghton reportedly jumped to his defence and declared that he would "rather offend Christian leaders who think Osteen doesn't preach enough about sin than the many non-Christians who are attracted to Osteen's message of God's love for them."[93] Excuse me Mr. Houston, of what use is this attraction of a message by a supposed Christian minister if it leaves non-Christians comfortable in their depraved state?

The consistency of Joel Osteen to his rhetoric confirms his unwavering focus to whatever Pelagian script he was trained from. Compare such to the great apostle of the Lord who would "neither use flattery nor put on a mask to cover up financial greed."[94] One who, when paraphrased, would write under the inspiration of the Holy Spirit that there is nothing adorable about you because every good thing comes from God; and that God gives saints grace to persevere because it's a myth that every day is going to be a Friday; and that declare all you want but if it is not God's will then it is not going to happen; and that you will never be a winner because Christ is the winner, therefore, you are more than a conqueror only if you abide in Him!

4. MANIPULATIVE TECHNIQUES

Manipulation is a devious way of achieving a goal by using an innocent person or people to one's own advantage. Whereas in most cases an innocent person is used to achieve the nefarious scheme and there are times when both parties are in cahoots, there is always a naive person or an unsuspecting crowd that is taken advantage of. In most cases, manipulation is a betrayal of trust especially through either abuse or a misrepresentation of power. Because manipulation is demonic in nature, manipulators hardly admit to their wrongdoing. Even when exposed or backed into a corner, they would rather find excuses or scapegoats for their wrongdoing. Manipulators can even wage propaganda with fake news in order to divert people's attention from any exposures of their untoward characters and schemes. Whereas manipulation in its blunt form can be expressed as cockiness disguised as confidence, manipulation in its subtle form can come clothed in false humility, even disguised as piety.

Laban is a classic example of a manipulator in the Old Testament. Through his shrewdness, he had potential to influence two generations of Abraham's family via an arranged marriage of his sister Rebekah to Isaac and arranged marriages of his daughters Rachel and Leah to Jacob. Laban exorbitantly profited from all these marriages. The son of Bethuel's egocentrism knew no bounds and even used his daughters as bargaining chips! Manipulators cannot stand being outmanoeuvred as Laban showed when Jacob got the better of him – he pursued his son-in-law and Jacob was only saved from further enslavement because the Lord was with him.[95]

God does not exist to do the will of men, but men should exist to do the will of God. In other words, God, in view of His perfection and unquestionable reliability, tests men because character is refined through challenges. But men should not test God. Therefore, attempts to put God to the test by demanding that He show wonders in order to be believed is manipulation inasmuch as creation itself is a wonder that evinces God's self-existence and unequalled supremacy. It is regrettable and very dispiriting when the flock of the Lord is manipulated by people who are otherwise supposed to be their shepherds and who should be exemplary in adoring and reverencing God.

On his second missionary travel, the Apostle Paul was accompanied by Silas when the masters of a fortune-teller in Philippi realized that the deliverance of this slave girl meant their source of income was also gone. They manipulated the city into an uproar by presenting an emotive matter with a xenophobic angle that these *Jews* were disrespecting the customs of the rulers of the day, the *Romans*. If the Gospel was threatening their financial wellbeing, then they would rather have it prohibited because clearly to them Mammon mattered more than God. Even when the Apostle Paul was accompanied by Gaius and Aristarchus to proclaim Christ in Ephesus, the silversmith Demetrius manipulated the Ephesians by presenting his concern for financial loss owing to the conversion of the Ephesians to Christianity. While his concern was financial wellbeing, he disguised his greediness by emotively presenting it veiled as a concern for the religious wellbeing of the city of 'Great Artemis of the Ephesians!' In a way, the courage of the mayor to quell the uproar by directing the silversmith to make formal charges if the missionaries had committed a crime exposed the real intent of Demetrius.[96] When critiquing the manuscript of this book, Professor Steve Zimmerman who authored the book *My Brother Philemon* added, "The great temple of Diana (Artimus) of the Ephesians is no longer standing. Despite the riot and uproar led by the silversmith Demetrius, it was destroyed. All that remains is one tall column with a stork's nest on top and a few broken pillars. I know because I was there and saw it myself! The gospel continued but Diana fell!"

Manipulative people are always self-centred. They may present their disguised scheme as beneficial to others but in essence, they are always looking out for themselves because manipulators love to control people. To the manipulators, people are essentially objects that should be used to advance their agenda. Ponzi schemes are always designed to look like they are beneficial to many people but in essence they are designed always to enrich the brains behind the scheme. Such schemes capitalize on the fact that despair makes people emotionally vulnerable. Former Secretary of State of New Jersey and now pastor of The First Baptist Church of Lincoln Gardens in Somerset, DeForest Soaries Jr, wrote: "Teaching that desire for more material possessions is a sign of one's religious piety is simply offering a justification for crass consumerism. Prosperity theology elevates greed to a virtue instead of leaving it as one of the seven deadly sins. Of course, it is much easier for clergy to preach this gospel when they are living proof that the 'system' works. Hence the celebrity-life lifestyles of so many religious leaders. The fact that the people most likely to do well in the prosperity gospel movement are at the top suggests that it is all an ecclesiastical pyramid scheme."[97]

Prosperity preachers are a unique class of manipulators. When Scripture talks of abundant life, prosperity preachers do not exegete that it refers to a believer's spiritual and eternal life accomplished and fulfilled by Christ but allege that abundant life is material prosperity. The prosperity gospel is a false promise of material wealth and perfect health based on a misinterpretation of the Bible. A metaphysical Christianity is no Christianity at all.

It is a disguised heresy, to say the least. Retired Professor Emeritus of Religion at Claremont Graduate University in California who specialized in New Testament Studies and Nag Hammadi Studies, James McConkey Robinson, remarked: "During the last decade, I've spoken with numerous people whose lives have been negatively affected by this unbalanced teaching on giving. The teaching has come from ministers who are using Scriptures on 'getting the return' to appeal to the Western materialistic mind-set. 'Just give and it will come back,' these ministers tell the crowds, with a fervour that convinces many listeners. They refer to a thirty-, sixty- and hundredfold return in a way that implies the contributor can expect to receive an immediate blessing – presumably so his or her debts can be quickly eliminated. The fact that some people's spending habits and financial practices should be drastically altered is not even addressed... Some ministers believe they are teaching the truth, and they may be sincerely seeking to help the hearer... My intention is not to accuse anyone of deliberately misleading or manipulating those whom they impact. But I have seen first-hand the unhealthy consequences of this type of teaching, and the manipulation breaks my heart."[98]

Televangelism indeed replaced tent evangelism and has the superior capability of reaching more people. Yet the growth of a church is not solely measured numerically but essentially according to healthy spiritual edification. Christ is the Gospel, and anything less than the Gospel can neither sustain nor save. It does not matter how trendy and exciting the prosperity message is, at best, it can give birth to happily deceived people who would identify themselves with a faith that they essentially know nothing about and are not interested in knowing about. To them, the politically correct message from their celebrity leaders is more than enough for them. Hot button issues such as the exclusivity of Christ in salvation, the eternal damnation of the unsaved and church discipline of unrepentant members have to be avoided or condemned. To consider anyone a sinner in need of salvation is forbidden because the masters and mistresses of positivism allege that everyone is inherently good, and the only regret is that man makes bad choices here and there. It is noteworthy to remonstrate that the 'Christ' of this worldview is not the historical and scripturally evinced Son of God. And if it is another 'Christ' then the Bible calls such a false Christ or an Antichrist.

In view of the interlink between the Greek term *apostasia* and its root form *aphistemi*, it becomes evident that apostasy is respectively not only 'falling away' but 'leading away' from an orthodox standpoint. In other words, there are some heretics who lead adherents in departing from true faith. Scripture is explicit that this apostasy, which some have aptly termed the Great Apostasy due to its distinctness and the use of the definite article 'ho' (the) in the Greek manuscripts, precedes the imminence of Christ.[99] You can only 'depart from the faith' or 'turn away from listening to the truth' if you were once part of that faith or once abode in the truth. In other words, these heretics were once part of orthodox faith but chose to depart in order to pursue something novel that identifies with the adherents' passions which the aforementioned Pauline theology calls 'myths, deceitful spirits, and doctrines of demons'. This means this new movement gains prominence because it mixes the orthodox with heresy. The Matthean text is clear that multitudes will not only be led away from the truth but will lead others astray in the process. When the Bible uses the phrase 'the apostasy' it does not only mean the aforementioned, but that it will be distinct in its pervasiveness. Note that all the cited texts harmoniously assert that this heretic movement emanates from the Church. If you are an impostor, it is only a matter of time before you show your true colours. It is one thing to be in error, but it is a different scenario altogether to be deliberately in error and deliberately misleading others because that is called deception. The Bible is clear that false teachers should be rejected and exposed. To sit therefore at the feet of a heretic is nothing short of endorsing the heresy. And we rejoice in knowing that Scripture is explicit that the elects abide in Christ and Christ alone.

The alluring power of the malevolent concoction called prosperity heresy is overwhelming to such an extent that even prosperity preachers end up speaking contradictions: the very people whose opulent lifestyles and heretic messages endorse prosperity theology can also be quoted here and there condemning the love of money or even saying scripturally sensible things relating to money. Yet, overall, the main content of their messages or their lifestyles is an open endorsement of the prosperity heresy. Furthermore, is the lightning speed prosperity preachers have in establishing so-called business seminars not telling? Because even if one is to be taught good financial management and end up prospering materially, it is not only the prosperity preacher who gets the glory, but those abundant 'breakthroughs' are required, if not commanded, to be harvested in the ministry of the prosperity preacher who is credited with having brought the anointing. Is it also not ironic that people saved from the system of the world are now being promised worldly prosperity in church? Truly in gold some trust! The sheer sense of entitlement in the prosperity movement is flabbergasting. The prosperity heretics speak as if they are entitled to the wealth of this world and God stands ready to do their bidding at the click of their fingers. God is humiliatingly reduced to an ATM. Author, editor, and adjunct professor at the Southern Baptist Theological Seminary, Jonathan Leeman, aptly summed up the prosperity gospel: "It's like a wedding between a Wall Street shark and a self-help guru, all decked out in the paraphernalia of a Christian bookstore."[100]

CHURCH MARKETING STRATEGIES

Other worrisome trends of the prosperity gospel preachers are the marketing stratagem and show-business techniques underdressed to be palatable to the secular clientele. The paperback titles are so watered down that a Christian struggles to identify them as Christian literature in a bookshop, especially considering that much of this anthropocentric heresy, when written by motivational speakers, must be classified under 'self-help' as if it is not the Gospel if it is not premised on the feel-good factor. Terms and phrases that may not be marketable to seekers such as 'sin', 'repentance' and 'Jesus' are replaced with politically correct phrases such as 'God is Love' or 'You Are A Victor!'. In lieu of spending time in the Word, in prayer and theological research, prosperity preachers would rather spend time being trained in the art of persuasion, voice projection, and fashion consciousness. Furthermore, to tap into the audience's emotions by creating an atmosphere of excitement is nothing short of manipulation. To their defence, prosperity preachers point at the orthodox missiology motto that 'the methods vary but never the Message' yet considering how they go neck to neck in competition with the world, it is an ostensible fact that they have to change the product to remain relevant in the politically correct market. Since generating the much-needed revenue to keep the Mammonish empire afloat means keeping the client satisfied with the product, it is the product that must undergo modification. The Jesus being marketed by the prosperity gospel movement is foreign to the Jesus of the Bible. The line between the unholy and sacred is so distinct that one cannot cross it without noticeable differences and consequences. Hence one cannot surely expect to get the coveted benefits of Mammon without meeting the terms and conditions of Mammon.

Is it not telling that virtually all prosperity churches are based in towns and cities where the working classes are easily accessible? If the intent were to win souls, why then shun the lost souls in the countryside? It comes as no surprise that every prosperity preacher craves for TV time because this Wall Street gospel thrives on publicity. The glaring manipulation of new prosperity churches mushrooming mostly in the metropolises is evidence that marketing teams are sent in advance to survey the challenges of a particular community. And – boom! – the prosperity preachers arrive promising to solve them! A social gospel should, at best, be the by-product of the Gospel, not its prerequisite or substitute. Therefore, to premise church purpose on material promises defies the meaning and essence of the Cross. Dear seeker movement, human needs are insatiable. Hence the moment someone with better techniques of commercializing the Gospel pitches next door, the same adherents will desert you. The Church is upheld and sustained by the Gospel in its totality. If you take away the offence of the Gospel in order to be politically correct what you are left with is a manipulation under the guise of religion, not the message of the Cross. Prosperity gospel adherents proudly point out that they left their traditional churches and their 'fire and brimstone preachings' for the positive message of the Word of Faith. In the Bible, a crowd and its overflow of prosperity gospel adherents followed the Lord for the free lunch of fish and bread yet when the offence of the Gospel stung them, they forsook Him.[101]

Whereas emotions can be expressed in worship through joyful celebrations or even weeping, our emotions neither change God's character nor His will. In fact, the ecstasy and emotional frenzy characterizing some gatherings of worshippers identifies more with occultism than an expression of faith in God. Attempts to claim evidence of the presence of God through sentimentalism borders on manipulation inasmuch as Scripture elucidates that the very fact that believers gather to worship Jesus evinces the presence of God – the very Christ who promised believers that He will always be with them.[102] Countless times we hear MCs in church services announcing, 'let's welcome the Holy Spirit'. Welcome Him from where? How did you even gather without Him? Who enabled you to gather then? Clearly, the misplaced understanding is that an atmosphere of excitement and tingling sensations confirms the presence of God.

Sensationalism and sentimentalism go hand in hand when an ill-equipped crowd is about to be deceived. Built on the warped folk theology of revelation knowledge, the titles of books and teachings by such manipulators must be sensational enough to create excitement. After all, nothing sells in an unconventional world more than controversy. Statements that are blasphemous and outrageous are continually made because they suit well the heretic narrative of manipulators who have a Gnostic claim of possessing knowledge not available to the masses. They speak of having audible conversations with a visible God and have an entourage of angels in submission to them when they utter these amazing revelations. Some prosperity preachers like Benny Hinn and Kenneth Copeland have not only gone on air to tell the world what God, in His visible form looks like, but have even measured His stature! Prosperity proponents preach and pause for the desired effect because their utterances are extraordinary. Indeed, the gaslighted adherents are so awestruck by such a 'spiritual dimension' that they cannot help but celebrate such 'kings and queens of revelation'. A prosperity preacher would aver that a congregation is not in tune with his so-called spiritual dimension if they are not as excited as they should be about his message. He can even quip that they are not responding accordingly because the revelation is too high for them to understand. Not wanting to look dull or unspiritual the congregates are manipulated into creating a sensational environment because such is what is considered spiritual by the manipulator and peers. Those who may not participate in the hype are not only condemned as unspiritual but are even warned that things are not going well in their lives because they do not have the right spirit. Condemning congregates who seem to be less enthusiastic comes as no surprise since even in their preachings, they slander ministers who disagree with their claims.

The intent of sentimentalism in such church gatherings is clear: people who think with their emotions hardly make sane decisions. It is not misplaced to point out that heightened emotions can even result in a person emptying their pockets at church even though bills await at home. Even the world wonders at scandals which time and again rock churches where worshippers are instructed to eat grass like cattle, and some are instructed to go shopping with tree leaves with the promise that the leaves will transform into banknotes at the till! Such brainwash is birthed in an emotionally charged environment where the leader is above reproach. This environment perfectly suits a manipulator who can easily brainwash the naive by tapping into their carnal nature with claims of bringing a word of prophecy regarding their needs. A needs-oriented church is ripe for deception inasmuch as a true church should be Gospel-oriented.

Word of Faith churches claim to have brought a certain level of liveliness to churches with the purported daily life applicability of their messages compared to what they consider to be the too laid-back stereotype of traditional church services. Yet the church service setup, music, message, and the level of excitement required in these services all confirm the intent of manipulating emotions. Remaining relaxed whilst others are clapping and jumping for joy can indeed be easily interpreted as not 'being in the spirit'. So is remaining standing when those around you are falling down being 'slain in the spirit'. Building excitement is a prerequisite to audience participation hence the answer to the question, 'How was the church service today?' is usually based on the level of excitement or ecstatic display expressed during the service.

Word of Faith ministers make it a point to expect to be applauded when they are sharing their messages. If the excitement is not reaching the level they expect then they ask, 'Can I get an Amen!' What sort of homiletics requires the speakers to ask for an 'Amen' from the congregation? Amen is a divine consent therefore requesting one to say 'Amen' when in essence one does not agree with the views you are expressing is manipulation. Such heretics are usually the centrepoint of the message they are sharing. Whereas servants of the Lord like John the Baptist would rather be of no significance but billboards where only Christ is glorified in their ministries, Word of Faith ministers are always the main characters in their presentations. Their billboards advertise themselves and Christ is only a footnote – if at all mentioned lest some of their 'non-Christian followers' may be offended.

CHARISMA

And personal charm is designed to work like magic in prosperity preaching because charisma is prioritized over character and integrity. To be a 'smiling preacher' is the much-needed magnetism because charisma is the ability to influence without the use of logic. Word of Faith leaders are consistent in their unconventional methods even, as earlier noted, to the point of interpreting Scripture. As far as Scripture is concerned, God judges a person by character rather than appearance. Yet Word of Faith values charisma over character hence they brag when comparing themselves to others rather than comparing their abilities with the grace God gives to minister inasmuch as there is no room to brag when it is God who gives the ability. Their untoward cause is further enabled by adherents who would rather put up with the handsome and impressive looking Saul, though rejected by God rather than David, the ruddy shepherd chosen by God. Nowadays pastors preach looking funky because such qualities are what unconventional societies consider impressive. Some preach with torn designer jeans and others with tight-fitting T-shirts exposing their tattoos as if they are going to a gym. Yet integrity should be a leader's badge of honour inasmuch as integrity is not perfection, but it enables one to be contrite when wrong and accept correction.[103]

Since their ministries are built on charisma, their image is essentially protected to such an extent that they assemble teams of marketing experts that work round the clock to protect and promote the brand particularly via social media networks. Indeed, the image becomes an idol inasmuch as it has to be moulded within the framework of political correctness in order to remain relevant to contemporary as well as non-Christian followers. For the sake of the Gospel, the apostles were no strangers to controversies and persecutions, yet these celebrity pastors would rather be mum where Christian apologetics is needed because such a stance would damage their impressive image. Or they would rather have a voice on a matter their marketing advisors would consider appropriate as far as marketing their brand is concerned. Only the Gospel message should impress, not a person's credentials or appearance. Yet the Gospel does more than impress – the Gospel transforms and continues to transform believers to be Christlike. The very fact that one would prioritize one's image over the Gospel confirms that one is using the Name of the Lord with ulterior motives. Furthermore, giving oneself the liberty to teach false doctrines confirms that such a person is not abiding in Christ because false ministers are always looking out for their interests to such an extent that their so-called positivism denies that people have a natural tendency towards sin.

Since charismatic televangelism and the megachurch phenomena are undergirded by the personality of the leader, it comes as no surprise that such ministries are built on biographical testimonies meant to evince the painful past this now prominent leader came from. Victimhood marketing stratagem works like magic in garnering sympathy from the audience. Yet ministry is never about our lifestyles but all about God getting all the glory. Even in testimonies, which should not become sermons because Christ must be the centre and meaning of the sermon, God must get the glory because it is His grace that enabled us to prevail against otherwise painful circumstances. Whereas sharing life experiences as a means of congregates relating to the preacher sounds noble, the essence of the Gospel is that congregates relate to Christ. His exemplary life is sufficient to focus our Christian walk upon. Indeed, abuse in all its forms must be exposed and we could write biographical tomes on the pain and painful circumstances we have endured in this fallen world but that does not change the fact that to build a ministry by narrating a story of a 'painful past' is nothing short of manipulative anthropocentricism. Christ must always be the essence, meaning, and centre of ministry. Always.

Prosperity preaching attacks the essential attributes of God inasmuch as it presents a malleable god who panders to the manipulative psychology of the greedy heretics. Professor James Goff ably points out that God is "reduced to a kind of 'cosmic bellhop' attending to the needs and desires of his creation" by this faith movement.[104] Spiritual gifting and miracles are not ends in themselves but are meant to bring glory to God, not necessarily fame to the minister. Yet messages of Word of Faith develop a strong, if not unhealthy, dependency of the adherents on the leader. Bear in mind that the impact of the message cannot last because it is designed with the gratification of the 'here and now' in mind, not the eternal perspective. The message is as good as energizing a child with glucose – the immediate effect causes the child to be very active and excited, but those energy levels will plummet within a short space of time. Since the message cannot last, one is required to depend more and more on the leader in order to be injected with more energizing motivational talk. Indeed, the opium of heretics.

Flamboyance comes as no surprise in a world where charisma matters above all as evinced by fancy titles such as 'Dr Apostle', 'Dr Prophetess' and 'Most Holy' … though some do not even have fruits of the gifting to show or were schooled in backyard seminaries that offer degrees not worth the paper they are written on! Another reason such church egomaniacs use such fancy titles is to try to present themselves as the creams of the crop inasmuch as the title 'doctor' is meant to show academic intelligence and 'prophet' or 'apostle' is meant to show spiritual supremacy because the explanation proffered is that the apostles and prophets are the cream of the crop in the five-fold ministry. Even to call themselves prophets is no longer enough! Some in Africa like the Malawian Shepherd Bushiri are titling themselves Major Prophets! Superfluous titles are meant to show the qualitative differences between megachurch superstars and the gaslighted adherents. It's a way of saying 'we are above, and you are below'. The fruits of the gifting must always speak better than titles.

Watching a prosperity preacher at work will dismiss all notions that they are chancers. Hence Scripture affirms that they are 'well trained in covetousness'.[105] To claim that humanitarian aid justifies prosperity preaching misses the point because God is not glorified in deception. Indeed material abundance is the buzzword of prosperity preachers yet the Lord Jesus explicitly cautioned believers to take heed and understand that one's life is not measured in the abundance of material possessions one has.[106] Cambridge scholar in New Testament studies and historical theology, Richard Bauckham, aptly comments on the prosperity preachers in the blueprints of II Peter and Jude thus: "'In their greed, they will exploit you with fabricated arguments' implies 'that the false teachers make a good financial profit out of their followers, who are taken in by their teaching and contribute to their support.'"[107]

Considering the scandalous firestorms both within and without the Church and the never-ending controversies that face prosperity preachers at every turn, as well as the Scriptural anathema declared on anyone who dares preach another 'gospel', why then are prosperity preachers so foolhardy in pursuing the heresy? Arguably then their intent has never been about the Gospel, the very Gospel they are strangers too! Their intent probably has been to establish a platform to parade ego and fleece the flock in the process. How can such covetous people leave a platform where multitudes have been asked to 'plant a seed' in order to 'activate' the faith to receive health, wealth, and happiness? Brainwashed adherents are required to come forth and testify on any promotion or financial increase that came their way after giving the 'seed of faith' – even if such an increase or promotion was substantially bound to happen in the corporate world.

Is it not telling that the primary beneficiaries of the prosperity message are its very proponents? Yet people who have been beaten down by harsh life situations insomuch that they expect nothing but a miracle to improve their lives fall prey to these church vultures. Paraphrasing the phrasing of the Lord, the Church is supposed to be 'in this world but not of this world'[108] yet prosperity heresy is assimilating the faith to Mammon. I vividly remember being approached by a man in a supermarket in Sunnyside, Pretoria (now Tshwane) in 2012 with a trolley laden with groceries. He then 'prophetically' declared that he saw in a vision

God blessing me in abundance if I paid for these goodies! He was carrying a book by David Oyedepo. Scam or presumption? LORD, is this what has become of our treasured faith! I was excruciatingly disappointed. Prosperity heretics are a contagious cancer that must be exposed in Church, even if it means naming names.

The message of the prosperity gospel is always proclaimed in a defensive mode with an unmistakable element of cockiness against traditional churches. This is not surprising considering that the establishment of the Word of Faith movement was alleged to bring newness to church life. The defensive mode was inevitable because Scripture is clear that departure from the orthodox standpoint would indeed cause divisions as the wolves would introduce an attractive heresy of "smooth talk and flattery designed to deceive the heart of the naive."[109] Old-fashioned churches are accused of being too otherworldly hence the Word of Faith movement is keenly focused on the here and now and whoever opposes the prosperity gospel is accused of preaching 'a poverty gospel'. Traditional churches are, at best, viewed as being in slumber and too otherworldly hence the movement claims to bring messages that are relevant and daily applicable. Yet it must be pointed out that the so-called relevant message focuses on psychological and financial wellbeing. That antithetical view of traditional churches and the deserved criticism of the movement set the prosperity preachers in that defensive and cocky mode.

Considering how most, if not all, prosperity churches are centralized on the charisma or gifting of the founder, it comes then as no surprise that one hardly finds accessible essential documents such as the Church Constitution and a concise Declaration of Faith. Whereas the formulation of doctrines is a Scriptural exercise that should be carried out collectively by a leadership since it enables people to understand what you believe in and, consequently join or reject your fellowship, in prosperity churches only the leader constructs and changes doctrine according to the unquestionable revelation he receives. Church polity necessitates that there be a board to hold all leaders to account but, as aforementioned, since the ecclesiology of a prosperity church centralizes leadership on the founder, not a collective, essentially the policies implemented even regarding assets mostly give ownership to the founder. If all the financial labouring ends up giving ownership to one person, what then is the purpose of everyone else contributing towards something that is not collectively owned for the glory of God in the first place? The leadership boards you find in prosperity churches are handpicked by the leader essentially because of obedience to his or her revelations. Some prosperity preachers have gone all the way to write 'modules' for leadership training which call these right-hand men of the leader armour-bearers. Bear in mind that in the Old Testament, armour-bearers followed their leaders without questions and when war came, they would put their bodies on the line for the leader!

Statement of Faith and Church Constitution are not mere documents: the former is doctrinally binding, and the latter is legally binding. Whereas the former should be accessible to everyone inasmuch as "can two walks together, unless they are agreed",[110] the latter should be accessible to all members, especially those in leadership, because it is imperative to understand the polity, financial management, internal and external audits, wage bills, assets and liabilities of an institute one belongs to. The work of the Lord should be that transparent. Therefore, questions should be expected, especially, in view of doctrine, those of a theological nature, and in view of the constitution, those of a legal nature. And when those questions arise, they should be answered transparently rather than becoming inimical to someone who asks questions that may ruffle feathers. It is only difficult to give access to such essential documents if something untoward is taking place, such as the self-enrichment of a select few at the expense of the rest.

ANIMISMS & PROPHECIES

Contrary to the silversmiths of Ephesus who lost business when their clients left idolatry by converting to Christianity where their magic papyri were burned, and in consideration of the occult practices being witnessed in some prosperity preachers' services in Africa, such as claiming to induce a comatose state and familiar spirits masquerading as acts of prophecy, it is not far-fetched to point out the probability of soothsayers and fortune-tellers switching their places by now holding a Bible and calling themselves Christian ministers. Especially in the face of prosperity preachers now taking their clients and promising them prosperity if they 'seed into the anointing of the man of God'. Demons are rebuked in Scripture, but our modern-day controversial prophets now have a dialogue with them. The fact that the so-called men of God are strangers to sound doctrine evinces that something more sinister is at play inasmuch as there is no way in Christianity one can have the audacity of claiming to be a servant of God without knowing the essentials of the very Word of God.[111]

Simony is now being celebrated in prosperity churches in the name of 'love offerings'. Congregates must think twice before inviting such and such a speaker because his spiritual gift is in demand. Therefore, one must be financially sound to be able to call such and such a speaker to come and minister at one's service. Controversial displays of power through what is purported to be a prophetic ministry, healing, and deliverance or motivational speaking has catapulted the unknowns into prominence. Whereas the Apostle Peter declared "To Hell with your money!" to the magician, and, by extension, any attempt to manipulate God for financial gain, in some modern cases one may as well say Simon Magus has managed to buy the gifts of God with money – as if spiritual gifts can be bought! In view of positive confession, it was a dismal failure for the Apostle Peter and the Apostle John to confess that silver and gold they had none because a man of God must always be loaded![112] Manly Hall, a renowned occultist and one of the world's leading occult historians, let the cat out of the bag when he declared: "... there is abundant evidence that in many forms of modern thought—especially the so-called 'prosperity' psychology, 'will-power building' metaphysics and systems of 'high-pressure' salesmanship — black magic has merely passed through a metamorphosis, and although its name may be changed, its nature remains the same."[113]

To 'seed' and expect a correlative return, as if it is some sort of investment, turns God into nothing but a slot machine. The sick who 'seed into the anointing' but do not get healed are painfully told by these religious con artists that they do not believe hard enough! Faith then is no longer God-enabled obedience to His will but a tool they use to get whatever they want from God. The demonic brainwash of naive followers is very unnerving especially in the face of empty prophesies, that are pronounced upon them year in year out. 'The year of breakthrough' comes and goes leaving the poverty-stricken still poverty-stricken. 'The year of possessing the gates' comes and leaves the fleeced followers still scrounging. Yet they remain within the deception because this heresy is as good as gambling – one just cannot get enough and keeps on thinking that another try will bring the big break. The last place one would expect to be abused is in church. Yet today we witness this massive abuse of souls who come looking for the Saviour. And those looking for something else come ripe already for deception. Prosperity wolves are doing more harm than good to the Body of Christ by fleecing the flock as well as by the ungodly scandals that come with their controversial and egocentric lifestyles. What profit is it to gain the world yet forfeit your soul?

Whereas prosperity heretics particularly in 'the land of the free and the home of the brave' have mastered the marketing technique of manipulating the flock of the Lord, their peers in the Third World have mastered the ability to carry out the technique in its crudest form. Words fail to describe the blasphemy being perpetrated particularly in Africa! There is no limit to the amount of deception the prosperity heretics employ just to hold sway the ignorant followers: from threatening curses to those who disobey 'the servant of God' to faking miracles that range from claims to induce a comatose state', trances, hypnosis, prophe-lies (read 'lying prophecies'), miracle babies, miracle weight loss, wearing their founders' charms in the name of anointed regalia, to claims that we are little gods so whatever God does so can we because we now have authority on Earth – not God![114] How blasphemies can be uttered cunningly with straight faces goes beyond the pale. From Eastern religions introduced to the Western faith by Quimby's New Thought to the New Age Movement, any occult practice which fails to be utilized in this Mammonish theatre of dreams is so … lucky! Prophets' bracelets and the so-called anointing oil have now replaced the hoodoo charms of the shamans in allegedly protecting the saints. Or rather, hoodoo priests have now reinvented themselves as prophets in the church. Speculation is now declared to be prophecy: to ask if there is someone with back pain in an auditorium filled with hundreds, if not thousands, of congregates is not prophecy but manipulation because chances are there are tens of people with back pain in such an environ; without shame, the manipulators would ask such a packed auditorium for someone with a name starting with the letter 'S' to come forward! The so-called anointing oil and bracelets do not bring any blessings, by the way.

Naïve adherents throng megachurch auditoriums and 'overspills' – a term applied to seating spaces usually under tents outside the auditorium that are meant to accommodate others when the auditorium is packed to capacity. They do not throng to sit at the feet of Christ and imbibe His word and glorify God. They throng to see the prophet with an expectation that when he 'speaks a word' to their situation then their lives will never be the same again. They have come for a breakthrough – for so is the word used for their expected victory – and their despair has pushed them to a point where 'whatever the man of God says' they will do. The despair of some even results in expensive flights particularly to Nigeria to see T. B. Joshua with the belief that just seeing him, even from the crowd, will be their so-called turnaround. Yet it seems no one told them that if you keep on turning around you will end up being dizzy.

Considering that Israel was meant to be a theocracy in the Old Testament, the role of priests was central to the wellbeing of communities. Priests and their assistants were to serve the people at the Tabernacle in Shiloh as well as at designated cities throughout Israel. During the lawlessness of Israel in the time of judges, a time when people disregarded the commandments of God and did whatever seemed right in their own eyes, citing lack of proper welfare for priests, one young Levite traded in his faith in God and ended up leaving Bethlehem to become a personal priest of a, possibly moneyed, idolater called Micah in Ephraim. He went as far as carrying Micah's idols with him as part of his ministry.[115] Just as the young rebel had reneged on his priestly duties and ended up being owned by an idolater, he did not find it hard to dump Micah when the tribe of Dan required his services – pronouncing prophecies even when God had not given him a word to declare.

Switching sides did not matter to him because his ministry was governed by material needs rather than upholding the commandments of God.

Just as Micah had a personal priest, and just as Baal prophets in Israel were employed by the king, therefore uttered words that were favourable to their paymaster, so are some so-called prophets nowadays becoming personal prophets of the moneyed. Hence, they speak nothing but material prosperity upon their paymasters – even when the latter is living contrary to the principles of God. In whose name do you pronounce blessings upon an unrepentant immoral person? Just as Micah and the wayward priest did not mind forsaking orthodox priesthood and replacing it with their profaned version, instead of repenting from their waywardness, the Word of Faith heretics would rather establish their own novel way of ministry and worship. Moving from one Word of Faith church to another can easily be considered a norm inasmuch as one is not really keen on knowing God but on accessing the goodies He is said to be ready to dish out. One prophecy upon another, Word of Faith prophecies have been proven to be false yet that has never stopped them from pronouncing more lies.

The prophecies of the servants of God in the Old Testament were unpopular to the Israelites because they exposed their sinfulness and stiff-neckedness in refusing to repent. Rather it was the false prophets and their lies who were loved because they condoned their lifestyles and lulled them into a false sense of security. The ministry of false prophets is motivated by fame and fortune. Yet if it contradicts the Bible then it is not prophecy. If it cannot be confirmed, then it is not prophecy. Any message of doom that leaves people in fear rather than having hope in God is not prophecy. If the fruits of their ministries and their lifestyles are not Christlike then do not follow them.[116] Only occultists chant mantras and decrees with a presupposition that the spiritual power of their 'positive confession' will physically manifest their desires.

Yet the disappointments in the prosperity services continue to grow particularly during the time designated for testimonies. Professional actors from Hollywood should learn a thing or two from the prosperity testifiers! Whatever miracle that has not been testified on is indeed lucky! The extremity of the play-acting leaves even some continuists ashamed. What is glaringly telling is the fact that virtually all the testimonies have to do with material wealth ranging from promotion at work to entrepreneurs' miraculous profits in business! Hardly will one testify on growing in the knowledge of the Word or thanking God for giving the grace to repent from worldly lifestyles. If you thought testimonies are meant to glorify God then think again because it is the 'papa', the 'man of God' who is celebrated by each of the so-called testimonies.

SEEDING & MIRACLE MONEY!

Again, I distinctly remember one particular 'Firstfruits Conference' where I was one of the invited delegates and participants, and one exciting and anthropocentric motivational speaker, a bishop of some sort, was, among other blasphemies, dogmatizing the deity of men by claiming that God was incapable of involving Himself in earthly affairs without the consent of man because man now had dominion on Earth! His grave error was to expect an affirmation from me when he asked "Amen, man of God?" "No!" I shot back from the VIP section where I was seated with other leaders. I was livid and wanted to address his famous heresies head-on when we took a break at the 'pastors' lunch' but reasoned against it when I realized that virtually all the leaders in attendance had Word of Faith theology. I was the bad apple – as his message made an about-turn and henceforth confirmed. He hammered home that too much theological knowledge snuffs out spiritual understanding. Of course, 'Firstfruits' was an eisegesis of the Feast of Firstfruits in the Bible but now it referred to the big bucks congregates had to give in envelopes if they wanted the anointing oil's big breakthroughs in their lives.

Whereas the 'seed faith' doctrine, financial partnership, and exclusive conferences for wealthy donors predominant in the modern-day prosperity heresy were essentially popularized by Oral Roberts, selling 'holy' merchandise such as prayer cloths and anointed oil were popularized by A. A. Allen. As if God were some cosmic Santa Claus, prosperity gospel adherents are indoctrinated to believe that the amount of money you give corresponds to the number of blessings you will receive. Nothing has been left to chance when it comes to getting money from the followers – from the eisegesis of the Feast of Firstfruits to threats of a cursed life by robbing God and emotional blackmail! The claim by these prophets of doom that failure to give God will result in His wrath upon your life makes believers give out of fear, not wholehearted devotion. In the late nineteen-eighties, Oral Roberts made a sensational claim that if he did not receive the millions he wanted God would not extend his life![117] Lynette Hagin, Kenneth E. Hagin's daughter-in-law, introduced a tithing convention adopted by many Word of Faith churches where participants raised their tithing envelopes in the air and repeated an offering prayer. The significance of divine wealth led churches to publicize tithing and to set givers themselves apart from the crowd.[118] Church attendees are squeezed out of every penny by making it a competition to give the biggest amount. And those who do not give, or do not give enough, are accused of being a hindrance by blocking the so-called flow of the corporate anointing to the entire body of believers.

63

The phrase 'expect a miracle', popularized by Oral Roberts and still trendy in the Word of Faith movement today, is a contradiction that misleads by a futile attempt at presenting predictability and otherworldliness. Roberts also coined the term 'seed faith'. A sign can be expected because it awaits fulfilment, but a miracle is a wonder known and shown only by God for His glory and pleasure. God indeed does miracles, yet miracles in themselves cannot evince the orthodoxy of a ministry inasmuch as even enemies of the Cross do miracles, albeit counterfeit.[119] Furthermore, the Bible is clear that prior to the imminence of Christ, false Christs, false prophets and the beast, the Antichrist himself, will mislead the world with powerful displays of miracles to such an extent that if it were possible even the elect of God would have been misled.[120] Biblical fidelity evinced in sound doctrine and God-fearing lifestyle are essential marks of an orthodox ministry. The Word, when properly understood and applied, has the power to transform lives. Hence it is called the Word of God. The elect of God cannot be misled by charismatic heresies and fancy credentials because Christ takes pre-eminence in their lives. Nothing moves them than the beauty of the Lord in His suffering and in His glory. Miracles of God cannot be products of heresy. We should work and be productive rather than laze around waiting for the so-called miracle money.[121] Your best life now? That is a lie from the lowest depths of Hell peddled by the arch-prophets of Mammon! It now looks like man does not mind living by bread alone.

Prosperity gospel adherents love to claim that they walk not by sight but by faith yet miss the point that the material wealth they are in pursuance of is by sight. To send your followers to go and touch whatever fancy car they want and claim it is not faith but presumption. And putting God to the test does not go without consequences. Hence some lack financial wisdom and 'seed' all money expecting a miraculous harvest thereby leaving the family broke and bankrupt. Contrary to the hypocrisy of grandstanding, the church starts at home. Some millennials grow up hating church because they cannot understand how a parent goes out of his way to please church leaders in meeting financial obligations, yet basic needs are not met at home!

Is it not a wonder that all the so-called prophecies pronounced upon the naive congregates seeding 'into the man of God's anointing' are all about promotion, to those employed, and enlarging territories to the seeding business Jabez? And those who do not 'partner with the man of God' or give their 'donations' are not going to enjoy 'divine connections and financial favour' but remain under 'generational curses'. Those who question the Scriptural soundness of these teachings are labelled as rebels who must be reprimanded or avoided. Discipleship is hardly Scriptural but rather a 'financial partnership with the man of God'. Ordination then is hardly about one's calling but about how unquestioningly obedient one was as an armour-bearer ready to see to it that the needs of the 'man of God' are met. Prosperity heretics declare that children of the King deserve to live like princes yet in no unmistakable terms the Lord Jesus warns that the deceptive pursuit of material wealth can choke out and render unfruitful the Word in the life of a believer. Whereas Elisha would heal for free, Gehazi made sure that he would enjoy financial returns for the healings.[122]

Whereas giving in the Kingdom of God is meant to be a voluntary and cheerful act of worship, prosperity preachers are very strict in enforcing financial regulations that in the end are beneficial to them. When you hear them instructing congregates to tithe you will be left with the impression that if one does not tithe then one is as good as unsaved. The emphasis is resounding to an extent that pales the complete work of Christ on the Cross in comparison. If seed faith theology means that what one gives to God will be given back by God literally tenfold or a hundredfold in one's lifetime then indeed the field which Joseph of the tribe of Levi sold should have been given back to him by God literally tenfold or a hundredfold in his lifetime since he gave all the money he got from purchasing the field to the apostles. But alas! Persecutions were the lot assigned the apostles who gave up their possessions for the sake of the Cross and the Apostle Barnabas was not spared either. Indeed, unless our righteousness surpasses that of the scribes and Pharisees we will by no means enter the Kingdom of Heaven.

The so-called seed of faith is so paramount that even the character or means of the giver are hardly questioned. The fact that in Scripture God would detail unacceptable offerings is intentionally given a blind eye to. As if all the seeding heresy that we have heard was not enough, on the Easter of 2016 prosperity pastor Paula White made headlines when she took the teaching to a whole new level: she asked her followers to give $1,144 per person which she claimed to be 'resurrection seed' that could deliver from spiritual death sentence! The televised presentation as usual begged for money in the name of 'donations'. True to form like all prosperity preachers and the so-called revelation knowledge that is exclusive to the anointed ones, White said this resurrection seed was according to the revelation God gave her from the story of Lazarus in John 11:38-44. And, as if resurrection life was not enough, those who would donate $1,144 were further promised prayer cloths that would be points of contact between the person and White's anointing for healing. She said, "There's someone that God is speaking to, to click on the donation button by minimizing the screen. And when you do to sow $1,144.It is not often I ask very specifically but God has instructed me, and I want you to hear. This is not for everyone, but this is for someone. When you sow that $1,144 based on John 11:44 I believe for resurrection life."[123]

I never knew that we now have to pay to be resurrected. One could argue that the prosperity gospel succeeded President Obama's Marxism in the White House when Paula White became President Trump's spiritual advisor.

Speaking at the Indian Summer Festival in Vancouver in 2014, even the Muslim Reza Aslan, writer and scholar on religious studies said, "The fastest growing Protestant movement in North America is this movement that is referred to as the prosperity gospel. This is the gospel preached by people like Joel Osteen and T.D. Jakes – and when I say people, I mean charlatans. The argument of the prosperity gospel, if I can put it flippantly, is that Jesus wants you to drive a Bentley. That is basically what the argument is. That what Jesus wants for you is material prosperity, and that if you literally give, you will literally be given tenfold. That is not a metaphor, as it is in most churches. It is literal. You give me $10 and Jesus will give you $100. This is as profoundly an unscriptural interpretation of Jesus that exists. I mean, if there is one thing that is just so clear cut and just not open to interpretation at all of any kind when it comes to Jesus' message, it is his condemnation of wealth."[124]

The prosperity heresy trending nowadays is not necessarily new but old heresy repackaged. In the New Testament times of our Lord, Pharisees were the most influential class of religious leaders. In fact, whereas the Parable of the Two Men Who Prayed evinces the egocentrism of the Pharisees, the Parable of the Richman and Lazarus was a further indictment to the flamboyance of the selfsame Pharisees! They were powerful and showy religious leaders well known for their love of money, praise as well as fancy and distinguishing titles to such an extent that 'the seven woes' pronounced on them, as well as the scribes, by the Lord exposed and explained the kind of leaders they had become to Israel. The stingy and covetous leaders loved VIP seats at banquets and would put on a show of piety with long prayers just to disguise their greedy intent of even manipulating widows out of their properties!

Leaders who were meant to be the guardians of the faith were now nullifying the Word of God with their oral traditions. Ironically, such religious leaders were keen on questioning the authority of any new teacher in town! Some of the strong indictments include the fact that instead of celebrating over a proselyte, the painful reality is that such a convert was going to be turned into a worse deceiver than the deceivers who converted him because of their corrupted Pharisaical theology! Their love for money was so insatiable that they would recommend a person to swear by the gold of the Temple rather than God's Temple which could make the gold sacred! And they would recommend a person to swear by the gifts on the altar rather than the altar that makes the gift sacred! They were precise in giving ten percent of their income yet profaned an otherwise frabjous tithing principle of storing treasure in the incorruptible Kingdom of God by giving a blind eye to weightier aspects of the Law such as justice, mercy, and faith! Neo-evangelicals who advocate for a politically correct form of Christian apologetics may as well take heed in noticing that the Seven Woes are arguably the strongest indictment Jesus used to defend the faith. At least one Pharisee, a member of the Sanhedrin, called Nicodemus probably repented as evinced by the fact that he could openly defend Jesus in the Sanhedrin.[125]

Virtually no church is spared from the nuanced dangers of the prosperity gospel. There is uproar in America when churches, including some mainstream churches, get federal loans. The understanding is that the borrower becomes a slave to the lender. Therefore, when Caesar is the lender, and a church is borrowing then shekels have the potential of becoming shackles. Nevertheless, within Protestantism, the prosperity gospel thrives mostly among non-denominational and independent churches as well as in some Charismatic and Pentecostal churches. Reformed, Lutheran, Anglican, Salvation Army, even Adventist, as well as most Baptist and Methodist churches, stand against it.

It is noteworthy that neither the apostles in the Bible nor the Church fathers were affluent. They lived simple lives concentrated on bringing glory to God. The Eastern Orthodox Church, in tandem with the homilies on wealth and poverty by Bishop John Chrysostom, unequivocally condemns the prosperity gospel. Chrysostom was the Archbishop of Constantinople and an important Church father notable also in apologetics. Besides the controversies on indulgences, the official position even of the Roman Catholic Church on the prosperity gospel is of condemnation. The Reformers also were consistent in rejecting fancy lifestyles by ministers of the Gospel and exemplified by using material acquisitions essentially for the work of the Lord. The claim that sounding an alarm over 'such a minority group' is misplaced gives a blind eye to the influence of this movement especially through 'Christian' television channels. As a reiteration that believers cannot pursue and enjoy material things at the expense of eternal life, Church reformer and theologian John Calvin wrote: "He who commands us to use this world as though we used it not, prohibits not only all intemperance in eating and drinking, and excessive delicacy, ambition, pride, haughtiness, and fastidiousness in our furniture, our habitations, and our apparel, but every care and affection which would either seduce or disturb us from thoughts of that heavenly life, and attention to the improvement of our souls."[126]

5. IMPACT OF THE PROSPERITY GOSPEL

Throughout history, Christianity has been attacked both from within as well as without. Atheism, deconstructionism, and Secret Societies are some outside forces that have attacked the faith, and Gnostics, legalists and liberals have attacked from within. Yet this contemporary Christian subculture called the Prosperity Movement poses a unique challenge inasmuch as it attacks from within by posing as Christian, yet its main artillery is imported from the world by glorifying material wealth which the impoverished could only dream of but is now being presented as accessible if only they give and believe enough! The heresy of this metaphysical gospel is magnetic because it dances to the tune of our carnal nature. It contributes to the Great Apostasy where carnal audiences hoard sons and daughters of perdition that are held sway by their carnal desires: "For the time will come when men will not put up with sound doctrine. Instead, to suit their own desires, they will gather around them a great number of teachers to say what their itching ears want to hear."[127] Indeed narrow is the road to salvation yet wide and fancy is the highway to perdition.

Dave Hunt, Christian apologist, and T. A. McMahon, executive director of The Berean Call ministry, wrote: "Two parallel developments over the last 20 years have set the stage for an astonishing partnership that is just now emerging. On the one hand, there has been the exponential growth of the Positive Mental Attitude movement in the secular world. At the same time, the fastest-growing movement within the church has involved two distinct but closely related factions: the Peale/ Schuller Positive Possibility thinkers, with their roots in New Thought, and the Hagin/Copeland Positive Confession and Word of Faith groups, which have their roots in E. W. Kenyon, William Branham, and the Manifested Sons of God/Latter Rain movement. Peale and Schuller have long been popular speakers on the PMA circuit, and there has been little difference in what they presented either to Christian or secular audiences. This accommodation of the church to the world is growing at an alarming rate and has received unprecedented evangelical support from the formation of Success-N-Life Clubs, under the inspiration of Robert Tilton, the innovative pastor of Word of Faith World Outreach Centre in Dallas, Texas."[128]

Considering its predominance in Christian television, it comes as no surprise that most Christians, especially in the Third World, believe that prosperity theology is the real deal. They have hardly been fed on anything else, let alone the Gospel. We also grew up watching the Word of Faith movement till God gave us the grace to verify everything with Scripture. In her landmark thesis, *Blessed: History of the American Prosperity Gospel,*

Professor Kate Bowler explains: "In 1971, a cluster of independent preachers (predominately prosperity folk) comprised 42 percent of the top syndicated religious programs on television. In 1981, the total jumped to 83 percent. It effectively narrowed the scope of religious broadcasting, affording the Faith gospel a market-share that came close to a theological monopoly. Flipping from channel to channel on Sunday morning, viewers might worry that they were watching endless reruns."[129] We evangelicals, in particular, are also to blame for a laid-back approach whilst Word of Faith preachers monopolized Christian media with hundreds of free-to-air (FTA) television channels of warped theology. When those seeking to understand Christianity check Christian TV programming, they are going to find these heretic television channels and radio broadcasts. Most of them fall in love with what they are seeing and hearing because they hardly know the difference between sound doctrine and heresy. Just one good and easily accessible television channel premised on sound doctrine can make a world of difference.

Lars Wilhelmsson again remarked, "The Faith Movement, this fast-food American version of Christianity, which perceives God as a means to an end rather than as the end, unapologetically uses God for its own means. Yet it continues to grow at an alarming pace. Even though several books have been written and many sermons preached in the last decade to combat this surreptitious 'gospel,' it continues to infiltrate churches at an unprecedented speed. The leaders of this movement have been ingenious in selling their wares through the use of the latest technology and the slickest packaging of books and tapes. If in the early 1990's this created a 'Christianity in crisis,' as Hank Hanegraaff claimed in his book by that name, how much more is that claim true in the early third millennium!"[130]

The damage this heresy has caused in the Third World is concerning. Human capital goes down the drain when Christians who are supposed to be intelligent trailblazers become morons of church fraudsters. The prosperity heresy turns youths who could have been productive into brainwashed lazybones who expect miracle money. It also bemuses struggling Christians who are told that poverty and suffering mean you are outside the will of God. Considering the extent of impoverishment in Asia, Latin America, and Africa, it is then a no-brainer that prosperity preaching is attractive, particularly in these continents. Imagine telling poor people that instead of being worksome they can get miracle money simply by believing! Attempts at alleviating the welfare of dependency are self-defeating especially in view of the flamboyance that prosperity gospel requires. After all, attending a prosperity gospel service requires that one looks the part of someone materially well-off, even if it means living in mounting debts.

The term covetousness is derived from the Greek term *pleonexia* and it means greed. Covetousness is forbidden particularly in the Tenth Commandment of the Decalogue.[131] It is forbidden inasmuch as it is antithetical to contentment. And it is idolatry, [132] because one ends up doing anything to get money and wealth. Covetousness is constantly depicted as the bedrock of social evils in the Bible because the greedy accrue wealth by depriving and defrauding others. Thomas Aquinas, the Dominican friar and immensely influential philosopher and theologian explained, "Since the object of tradesmen leads especially to making money, covetousness is awakened in the hearts of the citizens through the pursuit of trade. The result is that everything in the city will be offered for sale: confidence will be destroyed and the way opened to all kinds of trickery: each one will work only for his own profit, despising the public good; the cultivation of virtue will fail, since honour, virtue's reward, will be bestowed upon anybody."[133] As earlier noted, the Lord Jesus warned us to beware of covetousness inasmuch as a person's life is not measured by the abundance, or lack thereof, of material possessions. What profit is it to gain the world yet forfeit your soul? Even money cannot satisfy a covetous person. Hence to the believers, particularly under persecution, the Lord exhorted them to keep their lives free from the love of money by being content with His provision inasmuch as, in His unquestionable faithfulness, He promised to be always with them. Shadrach, Meshach and Abed-Nego would rather be steadfast in their faith and be cast in the fiery furnace than worship Nebuchadnezzar's image of gold.[134] The heresy called prosperity gospel should be rejected. Theologian and writer John Stott aptly affirmed, "We have to have the courage to reject the health-and-wealth gospel absolutely. It's a false gospel."[135]

Envy is the very bedrock of covetousness insomuch as it is resentment that makes a person covet another's possession to the extent of going all the way, by hook or by crook, to possess that which one covets. Covetousness and corruption go hand in hand. In the Garden of Eden, Satan not only questioned but undermined Eve's contentment – the very contentment he lacked when he was still Lucifer as earlier noted. And behind money is the condition of a person's heart. Yet money does not only show where or who is a person's treasure but is also an act of worship inasmuch as its use evinces one's view towards God. As Professor Emeritus of Old Testament at Pittsburgh Theological Seminary, Donald Gowan, commented, "[The Old Testament] assumes throughout that there will always be some with relatively more possessions. This is no scandal, for wealth is to be prized as one of the good gifts of God (Prov.22:4). What is a scandal, as many texts have shown us, is when those who do not have so much are deprived of what is rightfully theirs by those whose consciences do not bother them? Perhaps the closest the Old Testament comes to a desire for a "Middleway" is put in individual terms rather than as a plan for society."[136] Yet arguably no instruction against greediness, particularly in ministry, could be more famous than the one the Apostle Paul gives to Timothy – even citing the elusiveness of Mammon which ended up ensnaring and shipwrecking the faith of those who were lusting after it.[137]

Dr Craig Blomberg is one of the scholars who nailed the subject on the head when he pointed out that "In 1994 it was calculated that the wealth of the world's 387 billionaires equalled the combined incomes of the bottom 45% of the entire world's population, or about 2.5 billion people. Yet already more than a decade ago, nearly 200 million of the world's poor professed some form of Christianity. And, to the extent that they become aware of our lifestyles through television or foreign visitors, they often wonder why we in the West seem to care so little about their plight."[138] According to Wikipedia, by 2006, three of the four largest congregations in the United States were teaching prosperity theology, and Joel Osteen has been credited with spreading it outside of the Pentecostal and Charismatic movement through his books, which have sold over four million copies.[139] Any Christian organization, publishers included, prioritizing money over Truth are worshipping Mammon as well.

BANKRUPTING PROSPERITY

The staggering level of Bible illiteracy in our time has really helped fan into raging flame this heresy. Visions, prophecies, and eisegesis by the leaderships that are meant to be obeyed unquestionably have authority above the proper hermeneutics of Scripture. The prosperity heresy is indefensible inasmuch as it is telling that even the world, under the full sway of Mammon, are shocked that church leaders have gone materialistic. Bear in mind that most of the vicious critics of the Prosperity Movement have been secular intellectuals. Heresy is supposed to be discerned by the Church since it is an errant interpretation of Scripture. Therefore, it should be telling that even the world has identified this lie.

In prosperity churches, godliness is not the determining factor for church membership, but the financial contribution one makes towards 'the ministry of the man of God' through monetary gifts or purchasing of products. Imagine the money a celebrity preacher with tens of thousands of followers makes by publishing a book! Bear in mind that purchasing the merchandise does not only express the need of the naive to learn but to show loyalty as well and therefore a sense of belonging. Here in Africa, the centrality of a prosperity preacher in a church goes as far as dogmatizing that whoever must share a message in his or her ministry should not only establish the message from the Bible but should quote especially from the selfsame leader's books as well.

Indeed, it is not a transforming sermon you expect to hear in a prosperity movement, but a motivational speech meant to stroke the ego of the carnal. The central theme of the prosperity preaching is anthropocentric – a materially rich person is the centre of focus, with God at his bidding. Charisma and motivational speech, not sound doctrine, indeed drive the Prosperity Movement. Psychology now replaces theology. Prosperity theology is a 'God helps those who help themselves' heresy repackaged as self-help and is easily identified with terms such as 'maximizing your potential', 'self-esteem', and 'love yourself'. Some of the arch-prophets of Mammon openly state that they will not teach about sin and Hell because it drives away people from their megachurches. Prosperity theology's so-called life applicability is carried forth at the expense of the otherworldliness that defines orthodox Christianity with tenets such as sin, judgement, and reverencing God. It presents a very low view of sin because a man in his depraved state is hardly presented as such but as someone good who makes mistakes. Hence message of prosperity preaching is nicknamed 'Christianity Lite' inasmuch as it avoids topics such as sin and Hell. The Cross is only preached *about*, not *on*, at Easter. And lip service is given to the sufficiency of Scripture because the prosperity therapeutic add-ons show that the Bible is essentially being considered insufficient.

Pertaining to this religious Ponzi scheme, Shayna Lear, managing director at the financial institute Insight Advisory Group who also holds a Master's in Divinity from Palmer Theological Seminary, warns, "The prosperity gospel has also become an export of America to the world. This distorted gospel is one of the largest and most tragic exports that America takes to the two-thirds world, especially Africa."[140] Sean DeMars, missionary to Peru on behalf of Decatur Presbyterian Church (PCA), Alabama further cautioned:"America is exporting a false gospel that is putting people on the A Train to an eternity of suffering, and you are part of the problem. Stop it. Stop sending wolves in sheep's clothing. Stop supporting them. Exercise discernment. You have supported over two hundred missionaries in the last fourteen years? Great! But what if fifty of them have been ravaging the people you sent them to?"[141]

The teachings and implications of the Word of Faith go beyond the movement. Considering the movement's predominance in the mainstream Christian media, it is not far-fetched to assert that the way the movement is viewed by the world has a direct bearing on the way the Church is viewed. The shame that is brought by the movement does not necessarily spare a Christian who does not subscribe to the Word of Faith movement because the world hardly makes distinctions of Christians in their judgements. To the world, these shameful things are what Christians do nowadays.

Perchance the Americans underrate the overwhelming power of their influence especially to the Third World. As evidenced in the fashion and music industries, here in Africa, this superpower is considered the magnanimous and impregnable trendsetter. If a heretic teaching grows and spreads among American churchgoers, picture its impact on ill-equipped pastors and their Bible-illiterate and impressionable congregates in the Third World! American preacher and scholar Rick Henderson aptly remarked, "In many other countries their resources are far fewer. Uneducated pastors, who are doing their very best and uninformed Christians, have this garbage pumped into their countries through radio waves and TV broadcasts. Because Joyce Meyer is endorsed here, she is trusted there. And she can afford to spread her message with the money she makes from American Christians who buy her books, CDs and who attend her conferences. Her influence is severely disrupting the church in the third world. Her teachings are the unfortunate starting point for Christians in the third world and it is birthing even greater heresies. The devastating reality that we have to come to grips with is that when we support her here, we support the churches she is undoing there."[142]

It is impossible to proclaim the prosperity heresy and uphold the doctrine of perseverance at the same time inasmuch as the former is a feel-good message which claims that being blessed means living in material abundance whilst the latter maintains that even believers face challenges. Pastor and founder of the Wisdom and Integrity Ministry, Miguel Núñez, wrote a very sobering article on this prosperity heresy: "The prosperity gospel is the result of the desires of a fallen heart, living in the midst of affluence, in a culture that claims, 'me first,' that values comfort, material goods, and choices, in search of the enjoyment of the life of the here and now. Once this non-gospel 'gospel' was born, it was easily disseminated due to globalization. Every means of communication and transportation has been used to carry the good news and this bad news. Today we have to say not only that ideas have consequences, but also that ideas travel quickly. We also need to remember that it is easier to disseminate a lie than to undo its damage."[143]

If only prosperity heretics could know the damage, they are causing to the integrity of the Body of Christ by lying to and fleecing the flock of the Lord![144] How shattering it is to counsel a victim of the prosperity vultures who was manipulated even into giving savings and life investments! Such people become disillusioned and dejected and easily start getting bitter towards God who is now accused of having allowed such things to happen. Dr John MacArthur, one of the outstanding critics of the prosperity heresy, ably pointed out the impact and consequences of this religious Ponzi scheme thus: "From the standpoint of the world, the average non-Christian that would turn that on...that is a good reason not to buy into Christianity. That is maybe the best reason. If I was a non-Christian, I would say, 'That is so obviously a scam, that is so obviously phony, why would anybody have anything to do with that? It is so counterproductive to the proclamation of the true gospel."[145]

Inasmuch as when the misled realize that the long-awaited promises are not coming to fruition, meaning they have been conned out of their hard-earned money, most of them will not only walk out of the heresy but will become bitter with the Church. Be very careful with the flock for which the Lord died. One cannot help but grieve and pray for misled souls especially considering that much of what is called 'Christian TV programming' is prosperity heresy being marketed by spiritual charlatans. To some, this is all they have known. They are yet to hear the Gospel. Regrettably, the church is now presented as an agent of impoverishment rather than the agent of social change through the Gospel. Prosperity heresy gives false hope inasmuch as it attempts to circumvent challenges and the need for determination under the guise of miracles.

The impact of the prosperity heresy should never be underestimated inasmuch as it is not only the Charismatics and Pentecostals that have joined liberals in being held captive by its magnetism. Even some evangelicals, fundamentals, and other mainstream churches are not spared from the impact of this Wall Street Gospel. For instance, Kirbyjon Caldwell is the Methodist prosperity preacher leading the biggest United Methodist Church in America. At times it could be easier to identify Christian communities that stand in support of this heresy than those that stand against it! But the truth is not a popularity contest. I remember sitting in church in Cape Town and the visiting minister from Johannesburg proudly admitted that he joined the bandwagon to save his church because those who had remained orthodox found their church attendants dwindling as the flock flocked to the new boys in town who were promising financial freedom and perfect marriages.

On what grounds can one justify living a celebrity lifestyle off poor peoples' donations? In the absence of Moses, Aaron is now ministering in the pulpit, giving in to the demands of the carnal congregates who want to sacrifice to the golden calf! Prosperity preachers are copying well from the pages of Israel of old in her carnal waywardness where "her leaders judge for a bribe, her priests teach for a price, and her prophets tell fortunes for money. Yet they lean upon the LORD and say, 'Is not the LORD among us? No disaster will come upon us.'"[146]

It is truly bewildering that such a perverse distortion of the Gospel which normally leaves the disenfranchised poorer and its rich proponents richer continues to draw crowds to its doorstep. If the material proponents encourage the poor to give sacrificially, why are they not walking the talk and sacrificing the riches they continue to hoard for the sake of the

Kingdom of God they claim to proclaim? Prosperity gospel leads to deeper poverty. Lisa Withrow, professor of Christian Leadership at the Methodist Theological School of Ohio, remarked, "What makes this gospel particularly dangerous is its propensity to claim innocence of any motive other than fulfilling god's will for human beings... The only reason some people remain poor is because they do not exert enough effort to promote their own success. They are considered lazy, ineffectual or misdirected and therefore 'unblessed.'"[147] Ron Kubsch, professor of Apologetics and Modern Theology at Martin Bucer European Theological Seminary and Research Institute, wrote concerning the prosperity theology: "Thus tends to victimize the poor by making them feel that their poverty is their own fault ... while failing to address and denounce those whose greed inflicts poverty on others."[148]

Unless the Lord, in His manifold wisdom, stops the movement, the prosperity heresy will arguably continue to thrive because it feeds on the materialistic nature of the world: with the Christian faith in Europe dwindling at a shocking pace and being replaced by the so-called reasoning of the Enlightenment Age as well as a thriving consumer culture; the robust and throbbing materialistic American Dream central to the American lifestyle; as well as the Third World craving for anything that can better its impoverished lives, the prosperity heresy surely has fertile ground to continue throbbing since it sets the hearts and minds of its victims on the things of this world rather than on the incorruptible treasures of the Kingdom of God. Scripture asserts that we die to the systems of the world, but the Prosperity Movement quickens the carnal nature to the systems of this world. Renowned Christian Apologete Ravi Zacharias writes, "We are living at a time when G.K. Chesterton's dictum has proven to be true. Meaninglessness does not come from being weary of pain, but meaninglessness comes from being weary of pleasure. We have exhausted ourselves in this indulgent culture."[149]

THE ESSENCE OF CHRISTIAN APOLOGETICS

Indeed Christian apologetics engages differing viewpoints respectfully. Yet it is misplaced to qualify the radical nature of Christian apologetics clearly revealed throughout Scripture for polemics. In essence, apologetics in Scripture is more radical than gentle especially in the face of unrepentant blasphemers. Our Lord and the Apostles never allowed themselves to fit within the confines of political correctness by being righteous, radical, and therefore relevant to the kingdom of God. Arguably no New Testament texts are radically apologetic in exposing prosperity heretics in Church more than Jude and II Peter 2. Whereas the Petrine epistle does also address the pervasiveness of the heretics in the present tense, it essentially declares in the future tense, 'They are coming!' And Jude declares in the present tense, 'They are here!'[150] The blueprints go as far as describing these Mammonites as 'ungodly men who turn the grace of God into lasciviousness', 'who run greedily after the error of Balaam for money', 'trees without fruit', 'wandering stars to whom is reserved the blackness of darkness', 'murmurers walking after their own lusts with mouths speaking great swelling words', 'false teachers who deceptively bring damnable heresies … beguiling unstable souls', 'dog returning to its vomit'…It is striking that these heretics are likened to Balaam inasmuch as the prophet-cum-sorcerer could only prophesy well for money. That very hypocrisy led to his ruin. Again, both epistles evince the link between love of money and love of pleasure which even result in sexual immorality. We have lost count of scandalous headlines featuring prosperity heretics caught in the web of sexual immorality. Just as the matter was imminent in Jude's time, to such an extent that he had to put aside penning other matters relating to our precious salvation to give radical apologetics against these Mammonites, so is the matter imminent in our time.

Rebuking heresies is not weaponizing the world against the Church but a defence of the integrity of the Body of Christ. Remaining mum on attacks on Christ by heretics for the sake of self-preservation robs God of His glory because Scripture unequivocally maintains that divisions in Church are caused by those who mock sound doctrine. Whereas the arrogant will remain indignant or even counterattack to protect the heresy that catapulted them to prominence, the prayer is that those who ignorantly follow such lies will repent. Servants of God should have no self to preserve because Christians die to self and now live for the glory of God.

Our Lord, the Apostles, the Church Fathers, and the Reformers could not think twice about rebuking heresies because the flock of the LORD must be protected. Whereas the Lord Jesus had to rebuke wayward scribes, Herodians, Pharisees, and Sadducees, the apostles had to caution the Church against the heresies and blasphemies particularly of Judaizers, the Nicolaitans, the Simeonites and the Gnostics. Fully knowing that the wayward priest Arius could either repent or launch an attack in defence of Arianism, and fully knowing that the wayward monk Pelagius could either repent or launch his own attack in defence of Pelagianism, Church Fathers went ahead, rebuked, and wrote apologetics tomes against such heretics because it is the duty of shepherds to protect the flock which belongs to the Good Shepherd. And the Reformers steadfastly stood their ground against unbiblical dogmas of Rome. Some gladly paid the price with their very lives because they had no self to preserve but lived for the glory of God. Ministers who would rather hold their peace to avoid backlash by opponents of the Truth are serving the LORD with ulterior motives. Prosperity gospel is a symptom of a disease and a demon of arrogance which mocks sound doctrine.

We should scoff at Relativism and proclaim the absolutism of Truth both in Church as well as in the public square.

THE BEAUTY OF REPENTANCE

What distinguishes children of perdition from misleading but ignorant teachers? Repentance! It should be encouraging to prosperity heretics when, for instance, Benn Hinn and Joyce Meyer made an about-turn and condemned the movement. It is also noteworthy that the Joyce Meyer and the Benny Hinn ministries cooperated with the investigation of the Senate Finance Committee of 2007 and both changed the ways of governing their ministries immediately after the investigation. Yet whereas both Joyce Meyer and Benn Hinn admitted that their prosperity preaching goes overboard,[151],[152] they still preach the same theology which undergirds the heresy. A good number of prosperity preachers do face that dilemma as is evidenced by their conflicting speeches. Historian Randall Balmer aptly observed Benny Hinn's dilemma pertaining to the prosperity preaching: "He at times has issued a public recantation of his 'health-and-wealth-theology,' only to return to it again."[153]

Benny Hinn could do well to learn from his nephew Costi Hinn who confessed to and repented of growing up living the American Dream of flying private airliners and staying in expensive hotel suites whilst ministering the prosperity gospel. Costi Hinn, now pastoring The Mission Bible Church remarked, "We were teaching things that were wrong. We were taking advantage of [people], exploiting the poor, using our greed, squeezing every last dollar out of people so we live the way they could never."[154] As a matter of fact, Costi Hinn does not only oppose his father's and uncle's twisted theology but went on to write a book exposing the prosperity gospel which he titled *"God, Greed, and the (Prosperity) Gospel: How Truth Overwhelms a Life Built on Lies."* He promised to give all the royalties to theological education as well as providing pastors and people exploited by the prosperity gospel with resources. Considering that the plague of prosperity theology has devastated Africa, he further donated a hundred copies of the book to The Central Africa Baptist College and Seminary to equip Bible students and pastors against this scourge. Indeed, this gesture is recommendable insomuch as the solution against heresy is to equip the leaders who, in turn, equip congregates with sound doctrine. To buck this trend of heresy, besides undertaking missions particularly in the Third World, it is imperative for orthodox seminaries particularly in the First World to offer scholarships to ill-equipped ministers of the Gospel in the former inasmuch as making seminary fees exorbitant is nothing short of Mammonism in itself. Yet it should be pointed out as well that to reverence God is more important than getting degrees in theology. For instance, Steve Furtick is a prosperity preacher with an M.

Div. from Southern Baptist Seminary. Equipping church leaders with sound doctrine should result in healthy churches.

Antony Thomas, an English documentary filmmaker and author, collaborated with Benny Hinn in 2001 to produce an HBO documentary, *A Question of Miracles*. But despite attending numerous crusades at which claims of miracle cures were made, Thomas was unable to confirm any of them. In an interview with the *New York Times*, Thomas said of his experiences with Hinn, "If I had seen miracles, I would have been happy to trumpet it. ... In retrospect, I think they do more damage to Christianity than the most committed atheist."[155] Even the very father of the Word of Faith movement, Kenneth E. Hagin, who was instrumental in the building of the prosperity preaching, later on, wrote criticizing the predominance of prosperity preaching as an attempt to "make the offering plate some kind of heavenly vending machine."[156] Even before his death, it is reported that he assembled a meeting of some of the leading prosperity preachers, including Kenneth Copeland, and chastised them for an excessive focus on money.

It surely should not come to the point of a jail term to realize that prosperity preaching is heresy, as was the case with prominent televangelist Jim Bakker. The prosperity preacher could only renounce prosperity gospel as heresy in his biography *I Was Wrong* after being defrocked for sexual misconduct, divorced by his wife, and imprisoned for fraud![157] In 1982, Jimmy Swaggart excoriated his fellow televangelists in *The Balanced Faith Life* for espousing prosperity theology and even retracted the message that he had espoused in *The Confession Principle and the Course of Nature*, published earlier that year. Yet whereas Jimmy Swaggart was the whistle-blower on Jim Bakker's sexual misconduct, he famously went on to be repeatedly exposed for sexual misconduct himself! These scandals had a plummeting effect on televangelism viewership. Even the renowned publicist of Pentecostal revivals, Gordon Lindsay, in his popular book ironically called *God's Master Key to Success and Prosperity*, conceded that the increasing focus on money had gone too far.

It is noteworthy and encouraging that, of all former prosperity preachers, Jim Bakker is now arguably the most outspoken in condemning the movement. In an interview by *Christianity Today*, Bakker confessed: "I began to look up all the Scriptures used in prosperity teaching, such as 'Give and it shall be given unto you.' When I put that Scripture back into its context, I found Christ was teaching on forgiveness, not on money. He was teaching us that by the same measure that we forgive, we will be forgiven."[158] He added, "I believe the harlot of the book of Revelation is materialism."[159]

In the Intertestamental Period, communities such as the Qumran shunned the pursuit of material wealth for piety and communal productivity. As earlier noted, Protestantism renounced flamboyant lifestyle in ministry. Anabaptists such as Hutterites, Mennonites, Amish and Brethren often renounced individual wealth as part of their protest to mainstream culture. And even within Roman Catholicism, monasteries were also established by priests who were opposed to their fellows' lavish lifestyles. Yet it should be noted that the Bible advocates for neither the prosperity gospel nor the asceticism of the poverty gospel expressed through vows of poverty.

When Roman Emperor Constantine adopted the Christian faith, to make his newly found faith attractive to pagans he also sought syncretism between the faith and Mammonism. Centuries later, whereas heresies and abuse of power became the spark plugs that set off the Reformation, Luther just could not stand the financial abuse expressed in the Roman Mammonism's jingle song of the Grand Commissioner for Indulgences in Germany, Johann Tetzel, who was presenting one's relationship with God as a quid pro quo transaction: 'As soon as a coin in the coffer rings, a soul from purgatory springs.' The scandalous Dominican friar would sell indulgences even for sins *yet to be committed*! Rome went on to amass material wealth from nations enough to build an independent state even claimed to be 'The Eternal City'. Cathedrals, including the rebuilding of Saint Peter's Basilica in Rome, were built through the sale of indulgences. Rouen Cathedral was even nicknamed the Butter Tower inasmuch as it was built from the sale of indulgences. Praying to 'Mary the Queen of Heaven' went digital in 2019 when the Vatican created an eRosary that could be bought for a whopping €99![160] All protestant reformers vehemently maintained that the sale of indulgences was nothing short of heresy since no amount of money can pardon one's sins.

Observing the materialistic abuse of almsgiving, Luther remarked, "Not what Christ has commanded, but what men have invented, is called 'giving for God's sake'; not what one gives to the needy, the living members of Christ, but what one gives to stone, wood, and paint, is called 'alms.' And this giving has become so precious and noble that God himself is not enough to recompense it, but must have the help of others, bulls, parchments, lead, plate, cords large and small, and wax in green, yellow, and white. If it makes no show, it has no value. It is all bought from Rome at great cost 'for God's sake,' and such great works are rewarded with indulgences here and there, over and above God's reward. But that miserable work of giving to the poor and needy according to God's commandment must be robbed of such splendid reward and be content simply with the reward that God gives. The latter work is therefore pushed to the rear and the former is placed out in front, and the two when compared shine with unequal light."[161]

In his book *The Protestant Ethic and the Spirit of Capitalism*, Max Weber writes that John Calvin and his theology, Calvinism, fuelled the 'spirit' of capitalism. This view is unfortunately misplaced inasmuch as capitalism was thriving prior to the Reformation. Furthermore, contrary to capitalism, Calvin maintained that the ultimate owner of the property is God since we are nothing but stewards. Therefore, the property should be used for the good of the public. Weber does not take into account that Calvin's doctrine on the total depravity of man is anti-sensual and that the doctrine of election evinces that lives then should be lived for the glory of God. Paul Schervish, professor emeritus of sociology and former director of the Centre on Wealth and Philanthropy at Boston College, and Keith Whitaker, former philosophy professor also at Boston College, remarked, "Most troubling is his [Weber] deduction of this argument from Calvinists who might have distorted their master's teaching rather than from Calvin himself. Troubling, too, is the effect that Weber's argument has had on the understanding of Calvin's thought. Many have taken it to mean that Calvin thought that if you are rich, you are saved: that possessing wealth indicates salvation. This clumsy claim contradicts Calvin's own testimony: 'The elect differ externally in this life in no way from the damned ...' Also, Calvin explains, faith may be subject to various doubts, but in the elect, these resolve into an inner—an unseen—tranquillity. Finally, Calvin argues that no external signs reveal election."[162]

Contrary to the Marxist utopia which claims that the panacea for the world's woes is worshipping at the golden calf of economy, Christian ethics maintains that even the best economies will bring pangs of pain as long as a man's relationship with God is not healthy. History as well as the bloody trail left behind by all facets of Marxism confirm that man sets himself in a self-destructive mode the very moment he relegates God to the periphery of anthropology or the utter darkness of non-existence. The impoverished, dangerous, and atheistic world view of Karl Marx focused on money, property, and gold. In Matthew 26:11, the Lord Jesus succinctly rebutted the utopia of Marxism by pointing out that they will always be poor people in this fallen world. Greediness is a sin – so is laziness. The so-called Progressive Christianity is simply another form of Marxism. A system of handouts creates unhealthy dependency and is not self-sustaining.

When, in 1977, the evangelical Ronald Sider tackled the issue of global poverty in his notable work *Rich Christians in An Age of Hunger*, it was not surprising that one of the outstanding critics of his work was none other than David Chilton who, in 1981, went on to publish an ill-informed and mocking polemic called *Productive Christians in an Age of Guilt*

Manipulators. It looks like the investor's guiltiness was tripped. Prosperity theology is anti-Christian but attractive because of its promises to bring solutions of worldly goodies to challenges people find every day. Happiness and victory are the catchphrases of the prosperity gospel. Yet this prosperity heresy is a futile and blasphemous endeavour to try to use faith to endorse covetousness in the name of Christianity. Scoffing at the redeemed because they may lack material wealth is to erroneously display a complete lack of understanding of what it means to be scripturally blessed.

Frederick Price charged: "[I want] to get you out of this malaise of thinking that Jesus and the disciples were poor...The Bible says that He has left us an example that we should follow His steps. That is the reason why I drive a Rolls Royce. I'm following Jesus' steps."[163] Prosperity heresy mocks the finished work of the Cross as well as the Lord's nature as a Suffering Servant. Jesus and the Bible are just footnotes of its motivational presentations. A materially rich Jesus marketed by this slot machine religion is utterly incompatible with Biblical truth.[164] Jesus was born in a food trough, and Joseph and Mary had to offer either a pair of turtledoves or two young pigeons to the Temple because of their poor social status, one that could not afford a lamb.[165] Neither Jesus' profession of carpentry nor some of His disciples' fishing profession were white collar jobs either. Equally misplaced is the claim that the presence of a treasurer among the disciples meant Jesus was materially rich inasmuch as whatever money He had was never meant for flamboyance.

Furthermore, if the treasurer of Jesus' ministry used to handle big amounts of money, why would Judas then opt to betray Him for *thirty pieces of silver*? Thirty pieces of silver in the New Testament were as good as a meagre single month's salary. In the Old Testament, thirty pieces of silver were equal to the price of a slave.[166] In the same vein, if His purse had a lot of money and He foreknew of His pending death, couldn't the money have been used to purchase His tomb – seeing that Joseph of Arimathea had to purchase His burial instead?[167] Matthew the tax collector and Luke the doctor could indeed be considered rich. Yet the fact that they left their professions to follow Jesus evinces that they preferred God over Mammon. Their ministries were antithetical to the ministries of the prosperity preachers who clearly do not think twice in choosing between God and Mammon. During His public ministry, Christ and His disciples depended on the hospitality of others as they ministered from town to town.[168] The lifestyle and ministry of our Lord was antithetical to the Prosperity Movement to such an extent that He warned Christians against covetousness.[169]

His apostles emulated Him by living a life fully committed to the Gospel even if the commitment meant suffering and persecutions.[170] Moreover, they pointed out that Jesus' voluntary surrender of His heavenly glory for the impoverishment of His life on earth was so that believers would have eternal life.[171] The prosperity gospel presents Jesus and the apostles as materially rich in order to justify its religious Ponzi scheme. Material wealth is never a prerequisite for serving the Lord. Though time and again they would receive gifts from believers, the apostles essentially focused on working for themselves.[172] A minister of the Gospel should maintain unquestionable financial integrity. Indeed, ministers of the Gospel should learn from the Apostle Paul's farewell address to the Ephesian elders at Miletus when he summarized his ministerial view on the money thus: "I have coveted no one's silver or gold or clothes. You yourselves know that these hands ministered to my *own* needs and to the men who were with me. In everything, I showed you that by working hard in this manner you must help the weak and remember the words of the Lord Jesus, that He Himself said, 'It is more blessed to give than to receive.'"[173]

MINISTERS OF THE GOSPEL

Charles Fillmore, another prominent American prosperity preacher and New Thought leader in the early 20th century made an amazing rendition of Psalm 23: "The Lord is my banker, my credit is good. He maketh me to lie down in the consciousness of omnipresent abundance; he giveth me the key to His strong box; he restoreth my faith in His riches; He guideth me in the paths of financial prosperity for His name's sake. Yea, though I walk in the very shadow of debt, I shall fear no evil, for thou art with me; thou preparest a way for me in the presence of the collector; thou fillest my wallet with plenty; my measure runneth over. Surely goodness and plenty will follow me all the days of my life, and I shall do business in the name of the Lord forever."[174] There you have it: Fillmore doing business in the name of the Lord forever! Again, God is left with no option but to guide Fillmore in the paths of financial prosperity ... if He knows what is good for Him. Ministers of the Gospel may as well critique such a prosperity eisegesis of Psalm 23 by pointing out the Good Shepherd surely ordained us to be shepherds of *His* flock who bandage *His* wounded sheep and keep the flock in the green pastures of sound doctrine. The lifestyle of a minister of the Gospel should be marked by godliness expressed in sound doctrine, genuine love for the flock of the Lord, simplicity, and contentment in the provisions of the Lord, not opulence and extravagancy. It is imperative to point out that claiming that a minister shows that he is blessed by mansions, private jets, helipads, and the like is a broad daylight mockery of the martyrs of the Cross. If a minister's integrity fails in handling the material wealth of this world, how then can he be entrusted to handle the far more valuable riches of Heaven in looking after the flock under his care?[175]

In his sermon 'Holding Fast the Faith' which was preached in 1888, at the outset of the Down-Grade Controversy, just after Spurgeon's censure by the Baptist Union, Charles Spurgeon questioned, "Doth that man loves his Lord who would be willing to see Jesus wearing a crown of thorns, while for himself he craves a chaplet of laurel? Shall Jesus ascend to his throne by the cross, and do we expect to be carried there on the shoulders of applauding crowds? Be not so vain in your imagination. Count you the cost, and if you are not willing to bear Christ's cross, go away to your farm and to your merchandise, and make the most of them; only let me whisper this in your ear, 'What shall it profit a man if he gains the whole world and loses his own soul?'"[176] Whereas, prosperity heretics fleece the flock of the Lord without blinking, is it not clearly telling that at the Apostolic Council of AD 48,[177] when Christianity was still in its infancy, one of the charges given to the Apostle Paul and Barnabas, which they were all too eager to perform, was to remember the poor? Whereas his gifting and impact could bring a great financial revenue for himself, the Apostle Paul rather focused on living an exemplary and simple life, proclaiming the Gospel and, in fact, generating money to help the Christians in Jerusalem devastated by a famine. Professor Dieter Lührmann, New Testament scholar and theologian, comments: "In Jerusalem and all the more now in his own new mission area around the Aegean, Paul could have played his trumps: rapidly growing mission areas and no doubt also an economic superiority in the new churches. But he does not do so because what matters is the gospel."[178]

John 10:11-13 evinces that labourers are servants of the Lord committed to the cause of Christ and hirelings are paid workers who cannot do the work of the Lord without considering good financial returns. Prosperity preachers "peddle the Gospel for financial profit"[179] hence greedy preachers must be held accountable for the management of church finances.[180] Fame, fortune, showmanship, and a megachurch have never been measurements of a true ministry. The fruit of the Spirit should speak more than the gifts of the Spirit in the life of a minister of the Gospel.[181] Prosperity adherents could easily read Scripture backwards inasmuch as the Kingdom of God is lived in the goodness, joy and peace of the Holy Spirit, theirs is a matter of eating and drinking because their "god is their belly". And, since they shamefully place God as secondary to their carnal needs, they become enemies of the Cross in the process and they keenly serve belly, their god, by flattering the naive.[182] Robert Murray McCheyne, an evangelical minister in the Church of Scotland, remarked, "If Satan can only make a covetous minister a lover of praise, of pleasure, of good eating, he has ruined your ministry. Give yourself to prayer, and get your texts, your thoughts, your words from God. Luther spent his best three hours [each day] in prayers."[183]

To safeguard church leaderships from opening doors to the infiltration of prosperity preaching heretics, pastoral epistles unequivocally maintained that an elder, also called overseer or presbyter, as well as a deacon, must have unquestionable financial integrity.[184] If a local church can have and maintain balance and checks on a leadership free from the love of money then the financial integrity of the church at large is maintained. A church leader held sway by greediness will do anything to get what he wants, even if it means preaching a message that pats on the shoulder the carnal nature of fallen men.[185] A lover of money is virtually a lover of pleasure inasmuch as greediness springs from carnal nature in order to satisfy that selfsame carnal nature. In fact, in the Parable of the Sower the Lord Jesus explicitly explains that lusting after the riches and pleasures of this world choke the growth and productivity of a believer.[186] And parables such as the Parable of the Pearl and the Parable of the Hidden Treasure highlight the incomparable value of eternal life over material treasures of this world. The love of money grows cold the love for God because one cannot serve two masters without offending one or the other. Hence our modern-day prosperity preachers continue to fulfil the impassioned scenario of the last days: "For many walks, of whom I have told you often, and now tell you even weeping, *that they are* the enemies of the cross of Christ: whose end *is* destruction, whose god *is their* belly, and *whose* glory *is* in their shame – who set their mind on earthly things. For our citizenship is in heaven, from which we also eagerly wait for the Saviour, the Lord Jesus Christ, who will transform our lowly body that it may be conformed to His glorious body, according to the working by which He is able even to subdue all things to Himself."[187]

Indeed, churches should look after their respective ministers of the Gospel.[188] Yet looking after ministers of the Gospel becomes Mammonish if the very ministers are now enslaved to the paymasters instead of bound to Christ. A church board should avoid unnecessary demands. Hence the need for a concise Church Constitution particularly in addressing matters such as salaries, assets, and budgets. The Apostle Paul preferred to work for himself. In this way, while he remained accountable to fellow ministers, he could speak the truth unhindered by the possibility of offending the paymasters. While he could have asked for financial support from the church at Corinth, he preferred not to in order to separate himself from the prosperity preachers who were peddling the Gospel for money.[189] He remarked, "You see, we are not like the many hucksters who preach for personal profit. We preach the Word of God with sincerity and with Christ's authority, knowing that God is watching us."[190] Hucksters were usually smooth talking but ill-equipped preachers who were keen on making money and cared less about the corrupting influence of their preaching on their audience. In reference to the false apostles, the *New Living Translation Life Application Study Bible* comments on II Corinthians 11:7 thus: "The Corinthians may have thought that preachers could be judged by how much money they demanded. A good speaker would charge a large sum, a fair speaker would be a little cheaper, and a poor speaker would speak for free. The false teachers have argued that because Paul asked no fee for his preaching, he must have been an amateur, with little authority or competence. Believers today must be careful not to assume that every preacher or evangelist who is well known or who demands a large honorarium necessarily teaches the truth."[191] Commenting on Matthew 10:10 renowned scholar D.A. Carson aptly points out that "the church does not *pay* its ministers; rather, it provides them with resources so that they are able to serve freely."[192]

We should indeed love, pray for and look after our leaders but it is unscriptural to follow leaders blindly. And there should be accountability on the management of finances in church lest the modern-day Judas Iscariots may take advantage and help themselves to the church purse. Judas would rather have the expensive ointment sold so that he gets the money under the guise of charity than have Christ glorified. Indeed Christ, the Bible, and God are mere footnotes of the greedy egomaniacs' agenda. Having money in the treasury would suit the needs of the thieving treasurer since he would always have access to it. The non-taxation of religious institutes should not give birth to manipulative fat cats in churches but should be a blessed opportunity for churches to broaden their base even in helping the needy.[193]

Our modern-day Zacchaeus's should give back to the flock they defrauded inasmuch as restitution is an essential part of repentance.[194] In 2005, Matthew Ashimolowo, founder of a prosperity church in England which preaches a 'health and wealth' gospel and collects tithes regularly, was ordered by the Charity Commission to repay the money he had appropriated for his personal use. In 2017, the organization was under criminal investigation after a leading member was found by a court in 2015 to have operated a Ponzi scheme between 2007 and 2011, losing or spending £8 million of investors' money.[195] Flamboyant lifestyles, even from leaders, must be frowned upon. Don't you know that some of your church members are going to bed on empty stomachs! Ministry must never be an easy way out when one has failed in the corporate world. Ministry is knowing with reverential certitude that God set you apart to nourish His flock in the Word. I was blessed one particular time I attended a church service in Camps Bay in Cape Town to realize that at the end of the month, all financials were transparently recorded and placed at the noticeboard so that every member knows exactly what their financial contributions were used for. Such transparency removes suspicion and encourages giving more inasmuch as money given is meant for the glory of God not for a leader to build his empire on Earth.

Dr John Piper remarks, "Here is the underlying worldview. A decisive turn happened in redemptive history when Jesus came into the world. The Old Testament was, by and large, a come-and-see religion, while the New Testament is largely a go-and-tell religion. That is why there is lavish expenditure in the Old Testament on the temple. *Come see, from Egypt and from Ethiopia and from the ends of the earth! Come see this expensive temple that we have built!* That's why wealth was seen so regularly as a sign of God's blessing. But that has all radically changed with the coming of the Son of Man, who had no place to lay his head and told us to go risk our lives to disciple the nations (see Matthew 8:20; 28:19). We are not living in Old Testament times. This is not a come-and-see religion, and Christianity doesn't even have a geographic centre. This is a go-and-tell religion. The coming of the new covenant has brought a revolution in the use of our resources. What governs our lifestyle now is the effort to show that our treasure is in heaven and not on the earth. What governs us is the effort to maximize our giving to finish the Great Commission and to love the hurting of the world. The New Testament is relentless in pushing us toward simplicity and economy for the kingdom and away from luxury and away from affluence and away from finery, including luxurious weddings."[196]

King Solomon, one of the wisest and arguably the richest man in the Bible, explained the observation he made under the inspiration of the Holy Spirit pertaining to the elusive rat race in pursuit of wealth which underlines the covetous philosophies of this world, the selfsame philosophy employed in the prosperity movement. In comparison to the simplicity of contentment, he wrote: "Whoever loves money never has enough; whoever loves wealth is never satisfied with his income. This too is meaningless. As goods increase, so do those who consume them. And what benefit are they to the owners except to feast his eyes on them? The sleep of a labourer is sweet, whether he eats little or much, but the abundance of a rich man permits him no sleep."[197]

ECONOMICS OF THE NEW TESTAMENT CHURCH

The Bible is essentially neither capitalistic nor socialistic in nature hence throughout both Testaments God establishes socio-economic ethics that were at variance with both philosophies. The phrases 'Kingdom of Heaven' and 'Kingdom of God' were synonymous, and both denoted a theocracy – a community ruled by the principles of God their patron. Contrary to the prosperity movement trend of plundering congregates for the material benefit of the prosperity heresy leader, the New Testament church had an economic interdependency in which those with generously shared with those without. And looking down on anyone because of their social status was severely censored.[198] The wealthy who wanted to make a show of the Lord's Supper by bringing fancy food that they would eat among themselves in the church were severely censored as well.[199] And the name of the Lord was glorified. The fruition of this selflessness is well encapsulated in Acts 4:34 which states that "there were no needy persons among them." The Bible is consistent in maintaining that material wealth is transient therefore should never be prioritized over eternal blessings.[200] And Acts of the Apostles is distinct in evincing oneness and sharing within a Christian community. Barnabas, Cornelius and Dorcas were among those praised for their selflessness. The one with two sets of clothes would share with the one in tatters[201] because church should be a refuge where brethren care for each other. Hence the Lord promised that those who forsake the world will receive a hundredfold of family and estate because there is voluntary sharing in the community of believers.[202] In reference to II Corinthians 8:13-15, Dr Mark Gornik comments, "Theologically, Paul teaches the importance of mutual sharing as part of God's 'manna economy'. In a manna economy, daily sustenance needs were met, making hoarding futile, all in a spirit of trust for God's provision."[203]

The self-sufficiency of a community of believers is a result of selflessness. Yet it is not self at work but God bringing glory to His name by enabling the church to yield to the influence of the Holy Spirit. Whereas Ananias and Sapphira attempted to deceive their Christian community by withholding money, the selflessness and compassion of Barnabas spurred him to bring all the money he got from selling his land to meet the needs of the community of believers. Commenting on Acts 2:43-47 and 4:32-35, William Larkin, professor of biblical studies, remarks: "We must understand, however, that the structure Luke points to is not coercive communism, that dispenses with the private property through once-for-all expropriation to a common fund. Luke never presents the system as a failure but rather sees all churches as living out not only their responsibility for the poor (Acts 20:5) but also their interdependence through caring for one another... Seen in this light, what Luke calls for is fully normative. With a mindset of unity, we will view our economic resources as available to meet others' needs. We will voluntarily, periodically supply our local assembly's common fund for the poor."[204]

Christians who merely wished the needy to be well when they were in a position to materially assist were openly declared hypocrites.[205] Commenting on James 2:14-17 Dr Blomberg again states: "Professing Christians today who have surplus income (i.e., a considerable majority of believers in the Western world), who are aware of the desperate human needs locally and globally, not least within the Christian community (a situation almost impossible to be unaware of, given our barrage of media coverage), and who give none of their income, either through church or other Christian organizations, to help the materially destitute of the world, ought to ask themselves whether any claims of faith they might make could stand up before God's bar of judgment. This is not salvation by works any more than the examples of Abraham and Rahab in James 2:20-25, but it is the demonstration of a changed life, a heart begun to be transformed by the indwelling Spirit of God, which thereby produces an outpouring of compassion for those so much less well off than oneself."[206]

Even at workplaces, rich Christians were instructed to treat their employees with dignity.[207] The New Testament indeed brings a counter-cultural ethic by not only outlining mutual respect and dignity between masters and slaves, especially in view of the equality in Christ,[208] but by also requesting the rich believers to assist the needy brethren without expecting anything in return.[209] Sharing as a community of believers did not mean the poor became too dependent on the rich inasmuch as this setup had an equal emphasis on working diligently and honestly in the corporate world because Christian ethics requires believers to be productive citizens.[210] Lazybones were scoffed at to such an extent that the Apostle Paul bluntly told the Thessalonians that the able-bodied who cannot work should not eat.[211] Poverty was never idealized in the Bible. Although poverty is usually an inherited status, it should not be regarded as a permanent state in the life of an honest and industrious person. Nevertheless, it is essential to empower the needy because in most cases the needy are victims of circumstances outside their control. Poverty is not good. Neither is greediness. The Apostle Paul admonished believers to work in order to break away from the welfare syndrome.[212]

SOCIAL GOSPEL?

God is unequivocally presented in both the Old and the New Testament as the defender of the poor and whoever takes advantage of the weak in community, the orphans, the widows, and the foreigners are heavily charged.[213] Even the God-fearing, including rulers, are required to show their godliness by defending the weak and making provisions for the disenfranchised.[214] We are encouraged to cap our expenditure by being lavish in generosity towards the work of the Lord, which includes giving good welfare to full-time ministers of the Gospel[215] as well as the needy rather than being lavish in hoarding possessions. Material prosperity as a blessing should lead to godly generosity. And children, who are easy targets of consumerism, should be taught that this generosity is an expression of faith, of appreciation to God the ultimate Giver who blessed us to be stewards of His creation.[216] Hence the Golden Rule encapsulates how we get and use our wealth as Christians. Furthermore, it is noteworthy that when the Lord ushers in the Millennial Kingdom He will also reward believers for their acts of charity towards the needy.[217] If God desires a just society where governments should protect the financially vulnerable, how much more does He expect His ministers to treat His flock?

Again, Dr Blomberg express, "The key to evaluating any individual church or nation in terms of its use of material possessions (personally, collectively, or institutionally) is how well it takes care of the poor and powerless in its midst, that is, its cultural equivalents to the fatherless, widow and alien. This theme pervades the Law, the historical books, wisdom and poetry, and the prophetic literature. People always take priority over prosperity. Those in positions of power have no increased privilege, only increased responsibility. The New Testament suggests that governments should promote justice, but it primarily emphasizes the responsibilities of the individual and the church."[218] God essentially had the poor in mind when He instituted the Sabbath Year, the Year of Jubilee, as well as when He instructed that the edges and corners of the fields should not be harvested so that the poor and the foreigner could glean! Sabbath Years freed Hebrew slaves who would have sold themselves to their kinsmen because of poverty. To save the freed slaves from the vicious circle of poverty, God commanded that they should not be released empty-handed and even established debt cancellation measures.[219]

Sincere governments, in conjunction with church councils of good integrity, should criminalize fraudulent acts that are foreign to orthodox Christianity. Church ministers' lifestyles should be audited. Scripture principle is that for those who were given much, much is required of them. Therefore, financially high-rolling Christians should surely be charitable. How one uses one's material wealth can also explain where one's heart is pertaining to material wealth. It is a norm that runs through the pages of the Bible that God materially blesses His people so that they should be generous especially to the needy.[220] Those who defraud congregates must be locked up. Whereas the Social Gospel should never replace the Gospel but, at best, remain its by-product, the Christian community will do well by running programmes aimed at alleviating socio-economic injustices, reducing crime, improving literacy, and social justice.[221] Just as the Apostle Paul instructed the Thessalonians, believers must be taught the merit of work and contentment in earning a living.[222] It is thus recommendable to have programmes facilitating empowerment of the poor to work and be productive to avoid being overwhelmed by the welfare list. Whereas altruism expressed in philanthropy and humanitarian aid is lauded yet if such does not emanate from agape, true Christian love, it holds no value before God.[223] Upholding the prosperity gospel may as well be as good as replacing the Gospel with the Social Gospel. Whereas Christian ethics evince the essence of working and being productive, fair treatment and payment at the workplace as well as good welfare towards the needy, yet such are never upheld at the expense of the Gospel.[224] The Jewish world of Jesus' time awaited a Christ who would bring about social justice hence most were disappointed by the otherworldliness of His message. Eternal life matters more than material riches. Above all, may Christ, not material prosperity, be uncompromisingly preached.

Is prosperity preaching then essentially doom and gloom? Arguably! The need to practically live out the faith daily by Word of Faith adherents is argued to result in an improved prayer life as well as time to spend reading the Word – though the eisegetical interpretation of Scripture by the leader regrettably usually takes precedence. Having a positive mental attitude is also good for one's health – although presumption disguised as positivism is very hazardous to both health and faith. Bear in mind that the Word of Faith heritage of the New Thought philosophy emphasizes that the law of attraction's effect on the mind impacts, transforms and shapes the decisions one makes daily. Some prosperity gospel proponents have claimed that their message has moved a lot of adherents from abject poverty to upward mobility but that is debatable especially in view of the fact that a person who depends on miracle money hardly makes an effort to improve academically and professionally. In fact, sound financial management is hardly prioritized in favour of the purported miraculous. As earlier noted, prosperity proponents themselves are not keen on sound doctrine hence the scorn they show whenever they mention seminary training.

Am I throwing away both the baby and the bathwater by criticizing the prosperity gospel and the Word of Faith movement? Should churches not talk about money then? Not at all! Critiquing should give a balanced assessment hence covetousness and fraudulent activities should be exposed and exegetical Biblical teachings on money should be upheld. Administration of a church requires money indeed, but Mammon should never be central to church life. The Gospel must always be central to church life. Believers should indeed be taught the essence of God-enabled diligence and honesty in business, the essence of productive work that results in providing for the family, putting aside savings, and supporting essential Christian undertakings such as missions and charity as well as giving proper welfare to the ministers of the Gospels.

To their credit, some African American churches created employment, materially assisted the needy, and ran successful businesses with the intent of alleviating welfare dependency on government. They were also vocal in addressing social ills. "This brand of Christian capitalism encourages African Americans to pool their dollars to invest in each other and their communities. Unlike a corporation that keeps its profits, church-based business enterprises enrich the neighbourhood by providing resources and much needed services like day care, soup kitchens, and substance abuse counselling."[225]

Christians have always been at the forefront of reaching out to the poverty-stricken as well as in establishing projects aimed at honing literacy and marketable skills. Even Roman Catholic liberation theology was a Marxist attempt to emancipate the poor from oppressive systems of governance. Black liberation theology is also preached in some churches particularly in America. And the Oxford Declaration on Christian Faith and Economics in 1990 was also aimed at addressing the inequality between 'the haves and have nots'. Nevertheless, the crux of the matter remains that the Social Gospel should never replace the Gospel. The extremity of prosperity preaching in a sense reawakened orthodox Christianity to reaffirm biblical ethics regarding money and business. It is a deception to give someone false hope and a false sense of security by making promises one has no power to back up. This false hope of breakthroughs and security turns prosperity gospel adherents into desperate, bitter, and even angry people towards God. The Christian's blessed hope is not in things, let alone material things. Christ is the eternal security and blessed hope of Christians. This otherworldliness scoffed at by the prosperity heretics is the very premise of orthodox Christianity.

7.   ANTIDOTE

The dominion God gave the man on Earth pertains to stewardship, not exploitation. Biblical stewardship means we are managers not owners hence generosity is an essential aspect of Christian ethics. The earth and its fullness belong to God. Judeo-Christianity ethics essentially evinces work as a blessing hence laziness is reprimanded. Stewardship gives man the responsibility to care for God's creation. The socio-economic woes bedevilling the world are not necessarily born of shortage but of fallen man's failure to be a good steward as is demonstrated by greediness and laziness. Emeritus Lecturer at the University of Aberdeen, Dr Kenneth Aitken ably points out, "If individuals and nations were thus contented, two-thirds of the world's population would not be living in poverty."[226]

The very God who created and sustains His creation gave resources which, when shared selflessly, are sufficient to feed the world. But because of Mammon, the few hoard and starve the rest. Hence the New Testament church gave the general panacea by evincing that a selfless community of believers could share to an extent that there was sufficiency for everyone. Whereas material wealth has no inherent value, Godliness is a treasure with eternal rewards.[227] John Hartley, distinguished professor of Old Testament at Azusa Pacific Seminary, commented:"Greed prevents a person from enjoying what he has, for it drives one to spend all one's energy on getting more. Conversely, if a person can learn to live with what one has and to take periodic times of rest away from work, that person has time to enjoy and appreciate what one has gained with a thankful attitude."[228]

BIBLICAL GIVING

God gives the ability to give. In fact, He enables Christians to get hence He does not require one to give what one does not have. The apostles maintained the same principle when teaching about giving.[229] This, in essence, means God's grace, not the command of men, enables believers to give. Countless times prosperity preachers proof-text that part of a verse which states "do not appear before God empty-handed" deliberately omitting the succeeding verse which clarifies: "all must give as they are able, according to the blessings given to them by the Lord your God."[230] When God instructed the Israelites under the leadership of Moses to build the Tabernacle,[231] He stirred the hearts of those who were generous to present gifts because such people give cheerfully. And, contrary to the warped theology of prosperity preachers, it is not only money that people can give in church. Moses asked craftsmen to come and build the Tent of Meeting. One can give one's talent, gifting, time, skill, or expert advice to the work of the Lord. After all, every good ability we have comes from the selfsame God. Again, contrary to prosperity preachers who hoard wealth while expecting everyone else to give sacrificially, when bringing gifts for building the Temple, King David became an exemplary leader by voluntarily giving his fortune to the work of the Lord. And the exemplary gesture did not go unnoticed inasmuch as leaders of families, tribes, army, and administrative officers at the king's court voluntarily gave towards the building of the Temple.[232] It is noteworthy that both the Tabernacle and the Temple were built from voluntary contributions. Furthermore, when the Jews returned from Babylonian captivity to rebuild the Temple on its original site in Jerusalem under the leadership of Zerubbabel, some of the family leaders voluntarily gave in abundance.[233] Even in the New Testament, believers in Antioch were moved by the grace of God to assist the brethren in Jerusalem who were affected by drought during the reign Roman Emperor Claudius.[234]

It is wrong to guilt trip or compel people to give. Being cheerful and generous in giving shows that a good steward knows that he is nothing but a manager of the good things he possesses because ownership is always with God.[235] Therefore, what a good steward has is used to bring glory to God. A believer who understands the privilege of good stewardship of money gives wholeheartedly, with gratitude to God for the honour to meet a need. A good steward continues to grow in the grace of giving. When there is transparency especially in financial management, good stewards are always willing to give. Having family members occupying all key posts in a church organization gives the impression that it is a family-owned business. The aforementioned church in Antioch did not think twice in assisting the church in Jerusalem especially given the fact that leaders of unquestionable integrity and generosity, Paul and Barnabas, were entrusted with delivering the aid. The fact that God enables believers to give shoots down the idea of competing in giving in the church. There is no such thing as a small offering as long as one is giving with an attitude of gratitude to God for having enabled one to give.

True giving does not bank on expecting something in return but is an expression of gratitude to God who gives the ability. The goodness of God teaches one to be a generous steward as is evinced by the value of what a person gives in accordance with the way God has provided.[236] Giving God leftovers is neither an attitude of gratitude nor an expression of good stewardship. Furthermore, during the time of the Prophet Malachi, God had issues with ungrateful Israelites who offered imperfect animals inasmuch as He had blessed them with healthy livestock. One's giving indicates who, between God and Mammon, is prioritized. The world sees money as a god to worship, believers should see money as a tool to render services. Scottish author and Christian minister George MacDonald remarked, "The heart of man cannot hoard. His brain or his hand may gather into its box and hoard, but the moment the thing has passed into the box, the heart has lost it and is hungry again. If a man would have, it is the Giver he must have. Therefore, all that he makes must be free to come and go through the heart of his child; he can enjoy it only as it passes, can enjoy only its life, its soul, its vision, its meaning, not itself."[237]

Inasmuch as selflessness is one of the principles in the Kingdom of God, He blesses us even with material wealth that we may also be charitable.[238] Financial contributions made in church are never meant for the self-enrichment of a select few but to bring glory to God through the advancement of His kingdom. Giving is never the issue because Christians are generous by nature of the new life. Even in their poverty, the Macedonians were generous enough to assist other struggling Christians![239] The theology of giving in order to receive more material blessings is faulty and manipulative inasmuch as God cannot be bought and being generous is indeed the nature of the Kingdom of God."Command those who are rich in this present age not to be haughty, nor to trust in uncertain riches but in the living God, who gives us richly all things to enjoy. Let them do good, that they be rich in good works, ready to give, willing to share, storing up for themselves a good foundation for the time to come, that they may lay hold on eternal life."[240]

BLESSINGS

The term blessing is essentially spiritual. Values of the world are temporary, and values of the Kingdom of God are eternal. Hence the term blessed denotes an enviable state of those who abide in Christ. Interestingly, all the five points of the priestly blessings do not promise material provisions but essentially emphasize the spiritual aspect of the blessings of God who is pleased, gracious, favour, protect and give peace to those who have a right standing with Him.[241] Obed-edom of Garth was not necessarily blessed because he kept the Ark of God when King David was afraid to have it in the City of David but because the Ark symbolized the presence of God as well as His covenant with Israel. In other words, in view of the Old Testament typology, he was blessed because he had the presence of God.[242]

Anything material can only be a blessing when it is a result of our right standing with God because material wealth in itself does not indicate the favour of the Lord. Contrary to the popular prosperity theology, the blessing of God is not what He gives us but that He is with us. Interestingly God would inspire His materially rich servants such as Abraham, Job, David, and Solomon to explicitly maintain that true riches were not material but spiritual.[243] The faithful should know that in this fallen world neither sickness nor poverty determines one's standing with God inasmuch as God can use even such circumstances to show His glory.[244] Yet in the world to come, there will be neither pain nor poverty nor handicap. The faithful shall have the best life then.[245] Not now. In fact, being blessed does not exempt one from trials. Yet even trials ultimately demonstrate the faithfulness and sovereignty of God because He shows His faithfulness to those who are upright before Him. For instance, while others would question God when they face challenges, the apostles, Peter and John, considered it a blessing when the Sanhedrin had them flogged for proclaiming the Gospel. And God confirmed His faithfulness by preserving their lives and by saving multitudes through their ministration.[246]

We are not blessed because of the material wealth we may have in our walk with the Lord. We are blessed because we have a right standing with God through the finished work of Christ at Calvary. It is not because of anything we did but because God found us in Christ before the foundation of the world and He predestined us for His glory before anyone knew of their status in the economic ladder of this world. When read in its context, Galatians 3:14 evinces that the blessings of the Abrahamic covenant, when applied to the Church in this life, are spiritual, not necessarily material. The fact that, regardless of their repeated failings, God continued to materially bless the patriarchs confirms the covenantal nature of the blessings. Dr Craig Blomberg cautions: "The wealth of the patriarchs must therefore be understood within its clear covenantal context. This wealth is tied directly to God's plan to give his people a special land. In the Christian era, in which believers do not live in a uniquely promised land, we must take care not to assume that wealth necessarily, or even frequently, represents God's blessing."[247]

Children emulate what parents do rather than say. Hence it is imperative to be exemplary in generosity. Children need to be taught the meaning of stewardship, charity, the essence of giving as well as the value of sharing. God should always take all the credit and glory even when parents narrate to their children the story of their material blessings. Above all, children should be taught about the faithfulness of God even in hardships because life is not measured in material prosperity. In such a way, children are not only being given a Scriptural perception that God provides all good things in life but that His character is not changed by challenges people may face. When the Israelites would gather for the festivals of the Lord, the whole family was required to attend inasmuch as children would learn about God throughout their history as a people. No one knows you better than your family. Therefore, there is no better place for faith to be expressed and grow than in the family. God, not money, should always be central in a healthy family life. And there should not be a difference between a parent's church life and family life. King David was indeed a man after God's own heart yet, notably at home, his lack of diligence in instilling discipline to his children led to sibling rivalry which resulted in incest, murder, and even bloodshed over his throne. Parents should not do the work of the Lord at the expense of family wellbeing.

A healthy family builds a healthy community, and a healthy community builds a healthy nation. If children are brought up with God-centred morals and ethics on selflessness, indeed such people will be blessed. What a blessing when faith is preserved through family generations: the Christian faith of Lois was passed on to her daughter Eunice who, in turn, passed it on to her son Timothy who served the Lord with the Apostles and became a second-generation Christian leader in the early church![248]

Whereas churches should care for their disenfranchised elderly, handicapped, and orphaned members especially in countries lacking government welfare, pensions, life insurances and other social securities, working children can look after their parents and some needy relatives. Churches should instruct the able-bodied to work because idleness is a sin. Our Christian responsibilities start at home. And the way a Christian couple looks after their parents is a good learning point for the children. Even as He hung upon the Cross, our Lord still sought Mary's welfare by entrusting her to the care of the Apostle John. Unlike the Pharisaical tradition which the Lord rebuked, of circumventing one's responsibility towards one's parents' welfare through Corban, working Christians cannot avoid looking after needy parents by giving that money to church instead! The Fifth Commandment instructs children to look up to and look after their parents. God promised blessings of long life to children who honour these instruments that He used in giving children life because grounded and loved children make better choices in life. Consequently, disrespecting parents had, and still has, its own challenges because it meant disrespecting God who delegated such authority.[249]

It is also imperative to pay taxes as well as have sound financial planning such as savings, investments, and insurance.[250] Yet our hope should not be in Mammon but in God. Financial literacy is essential especially to good stewards lest lives wallow in debts brought by the illusive Mammon. Pastime is an end to a non-believer yet to a believer family pastime is a refreshing enjoyment as well as an opportunity of expressing appreciation to God who blesses us every day with the gift of life. Long-lasting happiness and true joy are found only in Christ hence believers should be content with abiding in Him. No moth or rust can destroy treasures stored in His kingdom. "Keep your lives free from the love of money and be content with what you have, because God has said, 'Never will I leave you; never will I forsake you.'"[251]

The Bible has sound advice relating to the management of wealth and money: whereas Proverbs 13:11 asserts that money found by dishonest means will not last compared to money accumulated little by little in an honest manner, Proverbs 17:16

continues in the same vein by questioning the use of money in the hands of a person lacking wisdom on managing finances. Indeed, financial success is hampered when a person has growing bills and fails to cap unnecessary expenses. Scripture does not encourage competing with but loving thy neighbour. Your neighbour's achievements, born of wise stewardship and impeccable industry, should motivate you that realistic goals are achievable rather than turn you green with envy.

The vitality of a church has never been the megachurch but its grassroots. The fellowship of a local community of believers has vital aspects that cannot be found in televangelism and megachurch trends, such as fostering growth, accountability, and discipleship. The former should not be established at the expense of but on the foundation of the latter. Indeed, let there be a full storehouse at the local church so that even material needs of the needy are met. Let the orphans, widows, and stranded sojourners know that God can provide for them even materially at the local church! In lieu of one prosperity preacher living extravagantly, let the church board prioritize supplies to the storehouse inasmuch as it is a good way of being relevant to the local community as well.

CONTENTMENT

Televangelism is indeed a great tool to reach multitudes, if only they are reached with the Gospel rather than being fed poison. The Gospel is the blessed and transforming message of the Cross. The suffering of Christ, the longsuffering nature of God in redeeming depraved man and the triumph of Christ over all powers of darkness are the reasons we have blessed eternal life. Human needs are met at the Cross, not in the accumulation of material wealth. Regardless of the theme or subject being handled, true preaching is centred on the Cross. At the Cross, we die to self, so that only Christ is exalted in our lives. In the prosperity movement, the self is pampered and praised, and Christ is only used as a footnote to cover the heresy. We cannot share in His glory without sharing in His suffering, and that suffering imperatively means distinguishing ourselves from the system of the world rather than trying to fit the mould of the world Christ saved us from. Suffering for Christ is a blessing because it builds godly character.[252]

Indeed, God heals sicknesses yet being sick does not mean the sick are His castaways. His glory is beheld even in one's infirmity. In this fallen world, not everyone is healthy but in Eternity there will neither be sickness nor pain. Even God's children who are sick in this world will be fully restored. What a blessed assurance! Contrary to the eisegesis of prosperity preachers, the abundant life Jesus meant in John 10:10 is eternal life, not material wealth in this life. Furthermore, again contrary to the piecemeal interpretation of the Abrahamic Covenant by the prosperity heretics, it is in the Millennial reign of Christ where the material aspect of the Abrahamic Covenant will be fully fulfilled, where Christ will reign over the entire land promised by God to Israel, where His elect, both Jews and Gentiles, will rule the nations under His command.[253]

A believer may be materially poor but is rich when well-nourished and continually transformed in the Gospel. In sharp contrast, a person who has abundant material possession but is a stranger to the Gospel stands impoverished before God. Pertaining to letters written to the seven churches in Asia Minor, the Book of Revelation shows a stark contrast between the church in Smyrna and the church in Laodicea: the former is poor in material wealth and underwent tribulations yet rich and steadfast in the Gospel to such an extent that even the blasphemers could not sway them; and the latter is ostensibly wealthy in material possession with a spiritual impoverishment disguised as lukewarm.[254] Laodicea may as well depict our modern-day flamboyant prosperity preachers and expensive infrastructures of megachurch and satellite television who consider growth through financial revenues and membership headcount yet are strangers to the Gospel.

The stinging woes of our Lord against the Pharisees ring true even in relation to this prosperity gospel facade: "Woe unto you, scribes and Pharisees, hypocrites! For you are like whitewashed sepulchres which indeed appear beautiful outward but are full of dead men's bones and uncleanliness inside. Even so, you outwardly appear righteous before men but within you are full of hypocrisy and iniquity."[255] Relating to the Book of Revelation, distinguished professor of New Testament and Greek at Ashland Theological Seminary, David deSilva, comments, "The churches cannot be allowed to believe the *societas'* definition of what constitutes desirable wealth. Only if they accept John's attribution of true wealth to the faithful who suffer economic hardships and social ostracism for the sake of the 'testimony of Jesus' will the churches survive the economic pressures that will rise along with the political pressures in the decades to come."[256]

Contentment, the very antithesis of covetousness, is the ability to be grateful to God for daily provisions, lest we trust in our strength if we have superabundant provisions. Contentment is when a Christian is productive yet neither greedy nor lazy. Indeed, we give to Caesar what belongs to Caesar, namely taxes. And we give to God what belongs to God – our very selves! Agur's exemplary prayer is in essence a summation of contentment: "... give me neither poverty nor riches but give me only my daily bread. Otherwise, I may have too much and disown you and say, 'Who is the LORD?' Or I may become poor and steal, and so dishonour the name of my God."[257] Whereas material wealth tends to make people worship money, poverty is stressful and exhausting as the poor spend all their lives indebted to the rich for survival. Poverty as well tends to make a person question God's ability to provide.

Yet a believer's richness incomparably surpasses material wealth because it is rooted in Christ. Hence the Apostle James exhorted believers that despite the challenges that they may face in this world, even in their disenfranchised state, they should celebrate that they are rich and highly positioned in Christ. Likewise, believers who are materially rich should thank God for entrusting them with an opportunity to be generous and be humbled in knowing that material wealth is temporary but riches in Christ are eternal.[258] Both the rich Christian and the poor Christian are objects of God's love and should find contentment in encouraging, assisting, and praying for each other. Scripture regards true material wealth as meeting needs and using the excess to help others. Such a social status contentment brought honour; hence, it was considered noble. This also explains why the avaricious were maligned because they were taking away the honour of other men by hoarding and leaving others poor. Furthermore, this view helps in understanding that the issue at play is not an unnecessary condemnation of wealth but greediness and laziness.

Pauline theology gives the panacea for the issue of material wealth by asserting that "Godliness with contentment is great gain. For we brought nothing into *this* world, *and* it is certain we carry nothing out. And having food and clothing, with these we shall be content."[259] Godly contentment is indeed the antidote to covetousness. Yet it is not only a blessing to be content in the Lord's provision, but it strengthens faith as well. Hence in the Lord's Prayer, we ask God to provide us with "daily bread", not lifetime provisions lest we end up trusting in our abilities. In the wilderness, the Israelites were required to gather manna sufficient for the day and wherever manna was hoarded the Lord would make it rot. God gave the Apostle Paul, in particular, grace to master contentment in all situations by understanding that material wealth cannot be compared to the glorious riches in Christ. Hence he exhorts "... I have learned in whatever state I am, to be content: I know how to be abased, and I know how to abound. Everywhere and in all things, I have learned both to be full and to be hungry, both to abound and to suffer need. I can do all things through Christ who strengthens me."[260]

THE GOSPEL

When a rich young man knelt before Jesus wanting to know how he could have eternal life,[261] the Lord's response was a great test of choosing between God and Mammon: since one's attitude towards materialism is a good indication of the depth, or lack thereof, of one's love for money, it became mission impossible for the young man to be selfless and part ways with his riches by sharing with the needy. As if salvation comes from good works, he had made an amazing claim that he had kept all the commandments of God since he was young. Ironically, knowingly or unknowingly, he had expressed the deity of Christ by calling Him good because only God is intrinsically good. Yet the young man would rather kiss eternal life goodbye than lose the riches which gave him a good dose of self-reliance.

The Lord's response, which was astounding even to His disciples, clearly expressed the impossibility of following God when we are cleaving to Mammon because the two are antithetical. The young man claimed to have kept all the commandments yet by idolizing wealth he was breaking the very First Commandment of having no other god besides God! And if the First Commandment is broken the rest will cascade as well. The test was not necessarily about selling all his possessions but about exposing the condition of his heart towards material riches inasmuch as the young man's riches were his very security and identity. The ethics Jesus was establishing were astounding to the disciples because the Pharisaical theology of their day claimed that material wealth was a sign of the favour of God. The Bible answers the disciples' grand question "Who then can be saved?" by emphatically declaring that no man can be saved by his works[262] let alone his material wealth! Hence what is impossible with man, either salvation by man's works or its modified version of synergism, which is salvation by fallen man cooperating with God, is possible with God who wrought salvation to mankind solely by the complete work of Christ at the Cross.

It is not the Gospel to present God as a Santa Claus who has no choice but to exist to bring material goodies to men. It is not the Gospel when man is exalted to deity status and God the Son is reduced to a demi-god. It is not the Gospel when the offence of the Cross is deliberately omitted from messages in order to fit the mould of political correctness. It is neither the Gospel nor the love of God to avoid calling out wayward brothers and sisters lest one be called a fault-finder. It is not the Gospel but a mockery thereof to assert that the essence of Christianity is to show that one is blessed by accumulating material wealth. Smooth talk or charisma is not the Gospel because the power to transform is inherent in the Word not in a person. Furthermore, the power of the Gospel is not evinced in ecstasy but in a transformed life which grows in Christlikeness.

The Gospel is indeed good news because it points us to the only Redeemer, evinces the nature and unequalled supremacy of God and promises an eternal life of peace and worshipful joy in the Kingdom of Heaven. Hence the otherworldly nature of the Gospel should always be central to its proclamation on Earth. Proclaiming the Gospel faithfully is the essential mission of the Church, either the good news is accepted or rejected. The Gospel is an offence to the world inasmuch as it is the truth and does not pander to political correctness. In view of the fact that the world is impressed by power, influence and wealth and in lieu of a conquering king who would subdue Rome as expected by the Jews or a philosopher as expected by the Greeks, the Gospel presents a Suffering Servant who is rejected, jeered, persecuted and crucified yet rose in majesty and ascended in glory as of the only Saviour and is indeed returning soon to reign forever! The Gospel presents an inconceivability by human evaluations of the Christ who alone fulfilled, and continues to fulfil to a T, all messianic prophecies. The Gospel presents life from God's perspective rather than man's depraved and self-centred point of view.

Dear prosperity preachers and adherents, my prayer and desire is that we repent. Growing up I used to be enraged and defensive whenever errors of my ways were pointed out. Till I learned through hard lessons that the person who truly loves you tells you the Truth. I am an introverted bookworm who loves the quietude of my little corner. But the love of God dares us to speak in the hope that some may repent. I pray for you because only the Holy Spirit can renew our hearts and minds. God loves you. Commenting on Job 22:18–22, John Calvin exhorted: "Let us walk always in the fear of God, rendering gratitude and homage to God for the goods we possess, knowing we cannot enjoy them unless it pleases Him to continue his grace toward us. Then riches will be a blessing, and like honours, delicacies, and the like, will not intoxicate men or put them to sleep, but rather will make them more vigilant in placing everything in God's hands."[263]

Indeed believers are rich. We are very rich. Having faith in God does not guarantee material wealth but it does guarantee the elect eternal life – which is incomparably greater than temporal possessions. Hence believers are very rich in Christ. "Since then, you have been raised with Christ, set your hearts on things above, where Christ is seated at the right hand of God. Set your minds on things above, not on earthly things. For you died, and your life is now hidden with Christ in God. When Christ, who is your life, appears, then you also will appear with him in glory."[264]

RECOMMENDED READING

- Bakker Jim, Abraham Ken, *I Was Wrong* (Thomas Nelson: 1996)
- Bakker Jim, Abraham Ken, *Prosperity, and the Coming Apocalypse* (Thomas Nelson: 1998)
- Barnes Sandra L., *Live Long and Prosper: How Black Megachurches Address HIV/AIDS and Poverty in the Age of Prosperity Theology* (New York: Fordham University Press, 2013)
- Craig L. Blomberg, *Neither Poverty Nor Riches: A Biblical Theology of Material Possessions* (NSBT 7; Grand Rapids: Eerdmans, 1999)
- Bowler Kate, *Blessed: History of the American Prosperity Gospel* (Oxford University Press, 2013)
- Bowman Robert M, *The Word-Faith Controversy: Understanding the Health and Wealth Gospel* (Baker Books, 2001)
- Farah Charles, Jr. *From the Pinnacle of the Temple: Faith or Presumption* (Plainfield, NJ: Bridge Logos Publishers, 1980)
- Fee Gordon D., *The Disease of the Health and Wealth Gospels* (Vancouver: Regent College Publishing, 2006)
- Wayne Grudem, *Business for the Glory of God: The Bible's Teaching on the Moral Goodness of Business* (Illinois: Crossway Books, 2003)
- Hanegraaff, Hank *Christianity in Crisis, The 21st Century* (Thomas Nelson, 2012)
- Hanegraaff, Hank, *The Osteenification of American Christianity* (Christian Research Institute, 2014)
- Hengel Martin, *Property and Riches in the Early Church: Aspects of a Social History of Early Christianity* (Fortress Press, 1974)
- Hinn, Costi, *God, Greed, and the (Prosperity) Gospel: How Truth Overwhelmed a Life Built on Lies* (Zondervan 2019)
- Jones David W. and Woodbridge Russell S., Health, *Wealth and Happiness: Has the Prosperity Gospel Overshadowed the Gospel of Christ* (Kregel Publications 2017)
- MacArthur, John, *Ashamed of the Gospel: When the Church Becomes Like the World* (Crossway Books, Illinois: 2010), Third Edition
- Maura Michael Otieno, Mbewe Conrad, Mbugua Ken, Piper John, Grudem Wayne, *Prosperity? Seeking the True Gospel* (Africa Christian Textbooks Registered Trustees, 2015)

- McConnell Dan R, *A Different Gospel: The Cultic Nature of the Modern Faith Movement*, Updated Edition Paperback (Hendrickson Publishers, 1994)
- Ramabulana, Makhado Sinthumule, *Church Mafia: Captured by Secret Powers, An Untold African Narrative* (South Africa: Makhado Freedom Ramabulana, 2019)
- Salinas Daniel, *Prosperity Theology and the Gospel: Good News or Bad News for the Poor?* (Hendrickson Publishers, 2017)
- Schervich Paul G. and Whitaker Keith, *Wealth and the Will of God – Discerning the Use of Riches in the Service of Ultimate Purpose* (Bloomington, Indiana: Indiana University Press 2010)
- Wolfgang Stegemann, *The Gospel and the Poor* (Philadelphia: Fortress Press 1984)

REFERENCES

1.   Matthew 6:24 NKJV.

2.   Dr Thomas L. Constable, *Notes on Matthew*, 2019 Edition. https://www.studylight.org/commentaries/dcc/matthew.html Accessed May 2019. Used by permission.

3.   Matthew 6:24, Luke 16:9, 16:11, 16:13.

4.   Craig L. Blomberg, *NeitherPovertynor Riches: A Biblical Theology of Material Possessions* NSBT 7 (Grand Rapids: Eerdmans, 1999) p.132. Used by permission

5.   R. T. France, *The Gospel of Matthew* The New International Commentary on the New Testament Series (Grand Rapids: Wm. B. Eerdmans Publishing Co., 2007) p. 263. Used by permission

6.   R. V. G. Tasker, *The Gospel According to St. Matthew: An Introduction and Commentary* Tyndale New Testament Commentaries Series (Grand Rapids: Wm. B. Eerdmans Publishing Co., 1961) p. 76. Used by permission

7.   Genesis 13:1-14:24, 19:1-29, Psalm 110:4, Hebrews 7:1-28.

8.   I Samuel 8:11-18.

9.   Exodus 20:3, 17.

10.   Hebrews 11:24-26

11.   Deuteronomy 7:25-26, Isaiah 2:7-8, Hosea 2:8 8:4-6.

12.   Haggai 2:6-9.

13.   Amos 4:1, Ezekiel 16:48-50

14.   Hosea 13:4-8, Amos 6:12-13.

15.   Ezekiel 7:19-20.

16.   James4:3-4.

17.   I John 2:16-17.

18.   Revelation 13:16-18.

19.   Taken from *Revelation 17-22* (Word Biblical Commentary Series) by David E. Aune, © 1998 p. 997. Used by permission of Thomas Nelson. www.thomasnelson.com.

20.   Ps. 37:16-17, 49:16-20, 73:2-3, Proverbs 15:16-17, 16:8 30:9, Ecclesiastes 5:10, Amos 6:4-6, Matthew 13:22, 19:23, I Timothy 6:6-11, I Peter 1:14-15, Revelation 3:17.

21.   Matthew 4:8-11.

22.   R. V. G. Tasker, *The Gospel According to St. Matthew: An Introduction and Commentary* Tyndale New Testament Commentaries Series (Grand Rapids: Wm. B. Eerdmans Publishing Co., 1961) p. 54. Used by permission

23.   Proverbs 14:20, 18:23, 19:4, 19:7, 22:7, 28:15.

24.   Matthew 6:31-32, Luke 12:13-21, Deuteronomy 8:7-20.

25.   Psalm 73:1-28, Mark 4:19.

26.   Proverbs 13:7, 18:23, 19:1, 19:22, 28:6.

27.   Proverbs 14:31, 17:5, 19:17, 21:13, 22:2, 22:22, 29:14, 31:9, 31:20.

28.   Robert Wuthnow, *God and Mammon in America* (New York: The Free Press, 1994) p.10

29.   Martin Hengel, *Property and Riches in the Early Church* (Minneapolis: Fortress Press, 2007) p.30. Used by permission

30.   Stanley Hauerwas, *Matthew* (Brazos Theological Commentary on the Bible), Grand Rapids: Baker, 2006) p.81. Used by permission

31.   Taken from *Business for the Glory of God: The Bible's Teaching on Moral Goodness of Business* by Wayne Grudem, © 2003, pp. 48-49. Used by permission of Crossway, a publishing ministry of Good News Publishers, Wheaton, IL 60187, www.crossway.org.

32.   Wolfgang Stegemann, *The Gospel and the Poor* (Philadelphia: Augsburg Fortress Publishing, 1984) p.63.Used by permission

33.   Sandra L. Barnes, *Live Long and Prosper: How Black Megachurches Address HIV/AIDS and Poverty in the Age of Prosperity Theology* (New York: Fordham University Press, 2013) p. 203.Used by permission

34.   Galatians 1:6-9 NIV.

35.   D. R. McConnell, *A Different Gospel: The Cultic Nature of the Modern Faith Movement* Updated Edition, (Massachusetts: Hendrickson Publishers, 1994), p. 3. Citing Kenneth Hagin, Jr, "Trend Toward the Faith Movement," Charisma (Aug., 1985), p. 67. Used by permission

36.   D. R. McConnell, *A Different Gospel: The Cultic Nature of the Modern Faith Movement* Updated Edition, (Massachusetts: Hendrickson Publishers), 1994, p.3. Ruth Kenyon Houseworthy, taped interview (Lynnwood, Wash., Feb. 19, 1982). Used by permission

37.   Albert Mohler Jr, The Briefing Part II: "The Problem with the False Gospel of Prosperity Gospel is not that it Promises More than the Gospel of Christ, but Infinitely Less" https://albertmohler.com/2019/04/24/briefing-4-24-19 Accessed May 2019.

38.   David W. Jones, "The Bankruptcyof the Prosperity Gospel: An Exercise in Biblical and Theological Ethics" https://bible.org/article/bankruptcy-prosperity-gospel-exercise-biblical-and-theological-ethics Accessed June 2019. Used by permission

39.   Sandra L. Barnes, *Live Long and Prosper: How Black Megachurches Address HIV/AIDS and Poverty in the Age of Prosperity Theology* (New York: Fordham University Press, 2013) p.199. Used by permission

40.   Creflo Dollar Ministerial Association, Become A Member cheymaximcreative.co.za/Stage/CDMANEW/join Accessed November 2019.

41.   II Timothy3:1-5 NKJV

42.   Craig L. Blomberg, *Neither Poverty Nor Riches: Biblical Theology of Possessions* New Studies in Biblical Theology, (Leicester: Apollos, 1999) p.78. Used by permission

43.   "Are All Prosperity Preachers Charlatans and/or False Teachers?"Got Questions Ministries,   https://www.gotquestions.org/prosperity-preachers.html Accessed July 2019.

44.   Gordon D. Fee, *The Disease of the Health and Wealth Gospels* (Vancouver: Regent College Publishing, 2006) Kindle Edition, Loc 28. Used by permission

45.   Scott Thumma and Dave Travis, *Beyond Megachurch Myths: What We Can Learn from America's Largest Churches* (San Francisco, CA: Jossey-Bass, 2007) p.2.

46.   Kate Bowler, *Blessed: A History of the American Prosperity Gospel* (New York: Oxford University Press, 2013) p.65.

47.   A Christianity Today Editorial, "Oversight Overstep: The government should not ask whether churches break God's laws" January 2 2008, https://www.christianitytoday.com/ct/2008/january/10.22.html Accessed June 2019. Used by permission

48.   Gordon D. Fee, *The Disease of the Health and Wealth Gospels* (Vancouver: Regent College Publishing, 2006) p.10. Used by permission

49.   Los Angeles Times, Part 2: "The Selling of a Church – Church Markets Its Gospel with High Pressure Sales" Lermanet.org/scientologynews/latimes/lat-2a.html Accessed May 2019.

50.   John 2:13-22, Matthew 21:12-13.

51.   Excerpted from "The American Dream and the American Dilemma: The Black Church and Economics," in *The Black Church in the African-American Experience*, Eric Lincoln and Lawrence H. Mamiya, pp.236-273. Copyright, 1990, Duke University Press. All rights reserved. Republished by permission of the copyright holder. www.dukeupress.edu

52.   Milmon F. Harrison, *Righteous Riches: The Word of Faith Movement in Contemporary African American Religion* (New York: Oxford University Press, 2005) p.135.

53.   Dallin H. Oaks, The Parable of the Sower, https://www.churchofjesuschrist.org/church/news/dallin-h-oaks-the-parable-of-the-sower?lang=eng Accessed May 2019

54.   Steven Harris, Book Review: "Reposition Yourself: Living Life without Limits" by T. D. Jakes, 9Mark Journal, Jan–Feb2014,https://www.9marks.org/review/reposition-yourself-living-life-without-limits-td-jakes Accessed June 2019. Used by permission

55.   Chuck Grassley, "Ministry Responses to Televangelist Review" https://www.grassley.senate.gov/news/news-releases/ministry-responses-televangelist-review Accessed June 2019.

56.   Conrad Mbewe, "NigerianReligious Junk!" A Letter from Kabwata, http://www.conradmbewe.com/2011/02/nigerian-religious-junk.html?m=1 Accessed June 2019. Used with permission of the author

57.   Ogunlusi Clement Temitope, "Prosperity Gospel Preaching and its Implication on National Developments" International Journal of Humanities and Cultural Studies ISSN 2356-5926 Volume 5 Issue 1, June 2018 p. 316.http://www.ijhcs.com/index.php/ijhcs/index Accessed August 2019. Used by permission.

58.   Taken from *Charismatic Chaos* byJohn F. MacArthur Jr. © 1993, p.281, citing D. R. McConnell. Used by permission of Thomas Nelson. www.thomasnelson.com

59.   Charles Farah, Jr., *From the Pinnacle of the Temple: Faith or Presumption?* (Plainfield, NJ: Bridge Logos Publishers, 1980) p.13.

60.   Lars Wilhelmsson, *The Gospel of Health, Wealth and Prosperity* (self-published) p.33. Used with permission of the author.

61.   Robin A. Brace, UK Apologetics, "3 John 2; What is the Meaning?" www.ukapologetics.net/08/3john2.htm Accessed May 2019.Used by permission.

62.   Rod Parsley, *God's Answer toInsufficient Funds* (Canal Winchester: World Harvest Church, 1992) pp.46-47.

63.   Judith L. Hill, PhD, "Theology of Prosperity, A New Testament Perspective" (Africa Journal of Evangelical Theology, January 28, 2009) p.43.

64.   David Bishau, "The Prosperity Gospel: An Investigation into Its Pros and Cons with Examples Drawn from Zimbabwe," p.75, International Open & Distance Learning Journal, Volume 1 issue (1), June 2013.

65.   Colossians 2:4.

66.   Romans 11:1-25, 16:25-27, Ephesians 1:9-12, Colossians 1:26-27, I Timothy 3:16.

67.   Genesis 3:5.

68.   Taken from *Christianity in Crisis, The 21st Century* by Hank Hanegraaff © 2012 p.109. Citing Morris Cerullo, "The Endtime Manifestation of the Sons of God", (San Diego: Morris Cerullo World Evangelism, n. d.), Audiotape 1, Sides 1 & 2 Used by permission of Thomas Nelson. www.thomasnelson.com.

69.   Hank Hanegraaf, "Word Faith: What's Wrong with the Word Faith Movement" https://www.equip.org/perspectives/word-faith-whats-wrong-with-the-word-faith-movement/ Accessed August 2019.

70.   Taken from *Christianity in Crisis, The 21st Century* by Hank Hanegraaff © 2012 p.395. Citing Kenneth Copeland, "What Happened from the Cross to the Throne", Fort Worth, TX: Kenneth Copeland Ministries, 1990, Audiotape #02-0017, Side 2 Used by permission of Thomas Nelson. www.thomasnelson.com

71.   Taken from *Christianity in Crisis, The 21st Century* by Hank Hanegraaff © 2012 p.XIV. Citing Joel Osteen, Discover the Champion in You, TBN, May 3 2004. Used by permission of Thomas Nelson. www.thomasnelson.com

72.   Isaiah 14:12-14.

73.   Frederick K.C. Price, *Living in the Realm of the Spirit* (Shippensburg, PA: Harrison House, 1989) p.29.

74.   J. Kwabena Asamoah-Gyadu, *African Charismatics: Current Developments within Independent Indigenous Pentecostalism in Ghana* (Boston: Brill Leiden, 2005), p.221. Used by permission

75.   David W. Jones, "The Bankruptcy of the Prosperity Gospel: An Exercise in Biblical and Theological Ethics" https://bible.org/article/bankruptcy-prosperity-gospel-exercise-biblical-and-theological-ethics Accessed June 2019. Used by permission

76.   Matthew 16:24-26.

77.   Bob Johnson, "Book Review: Break Out! by Joel Osteen," 9Marks Journal, Jan–Feb 2014 https://www.9marks.org/review/break-out-joel-osteen/ Accessed August 2019. Used by permission.

78.   Taken from *10 Lies about God: and the Truths that Shatter Deception* © 2009 by Erwin W. Lutzer p.8 citing Joseph Haroutunian. Published by Kregel Publications, Grand Rapids, MI. Used by permission of the publisher. All rights reserved.

79.   Taken from *The Faith of the Christian Church* by Gustaf Aulén, © 1960 p.105 Used by permission of Wipf and Stock Publishers, www.wipfandstock.com.

80.   Mark 13:20, John1:13, Ephesians 1:3-12, Revelation 13:8, 17:8.

81.   Kenneth Copeland, Our Covenant with God (Fort Worth, TX: Kenneth Copeland Publications, 1996) p. 10.

82.   David W. Jones, "The Bankruptcy of the Prosperity Gospel: An Exercise in Biblical and Theological Ethics" https://bible.org/article/bankruptcy-prosperity-gospel-exercise-biblical-and-theological-ethics Accessed June 2019. Used by permission

83.   Genesis 12:1-3, 13:14-18,15:18-21, Ezekiel 36:1-37:28, Zechariah 12-14, Galatians 3:1-14, Romans 11:25-27.

84.   Gordon D. Fee, *The Disease ofthe Health and Wealth Gospels* (Vancouver: Regent College Publishing, 2006) p.8 Used by permission

85.   Randall Stephens, The Wilson Quarterly, Book Review: Blessed: A History of the American Prosperity Gospel by Kate Bowler, "Holy High Rollers," archive.wilsonquarterly.com/book-reviews/holy-high-rollers Accessed June 2019.

86.   II Timothy 3:12.

87.   I John 2:15, James 4:4

88.   Job 4:7-9, 5:17, 8:6, 11:5-6, 15:20.

89.   Job16:2, 42:7.

90.   Isaiah 38:21, I Timothy 5:23.

91.   II Corinthians 10:1, 1:10, II Corinthians 10-13.

92.   Kate Bowler, *Blessed:A History of the American Prosperity Gospel* (Oxford University Press, 2013) pp.178-9 citing Joel Osteen, Conference Visit, "A Night of Hope," Greensboro Convention Center, April 18, 2008.

93.   Katherine Weber, Christian Post Reporter "Lakewood Worship Leader Israel Houghton Says Joel Osteen is 'Real Deal.'" https://static.christianpost.com/news/lakewood-church-leader-israel-houghton-says-joel-osteen-is-real-deal.html Accessed August 2019. Used by permission

94.   I Thessalonians 2:5.

95.   Genesis 24:1-67, 27:41-31:55.

96.   Acts 16:16-40, 19:23-41.

97.   Albert Mohler Articles: The Briefing "Black Churches and the Prosperity Gospel," citing DeForest B. Soaries Jr., https://albertmohler.com/2010/10/01/the-black-church-and-the-prosperity-gospel Accessed October 2019.

98.   James Robison, "Another View of the Prosperity Gospel," Charisma Magazine http://www.charismamag.com/spirit/spiritual-growth/906-another-view-of-the-prosperity-gospel Accessed October 2019.

99.   II Thessalonians 2:1-3, I Timothy 4:1, II Timothy 4:3-4, Matthew 24:10-11.

100.   Jonathan Leeman, 9Marks Journal, Prosperity Gospel (CreateSpace Independent Publishing Platform: 2017), p.72. Used by permission

101.	John 6:1-69.

102.	Matthew 18:20, 28:20.

103.	I Samuel 16:7, Psalm 25:21, IICorinthians 10:12-13.

104.	James R. Goff, Jr., "The Faith That Claims," Christianity Today, vol. 34, February 1990 https://www.christianitytoday.com/ct/1990/feebruary-19/faith-that-claims.html Accessed August 2019. Used by permission

105.	II Peter 2:3.

106.	Luke 12:15.

107.	Richard J. Bauckham, *2 Peter-Jude*, Volume 50, Word Biblical Commentary (Waco: Word, 1983), p.243.

108.	John 17:14.

109.	Romans 16:17-18.

110.	Amos3:3.

111.	Acts 16:17-24, 19:23-41.

112.	Acts 8:18-23, 3:1-10.

113.	Manly P. Hall, *Masonic, Hermetic, Qabbalistic and Rosicrucian Symbolical Philosophy* (Los Angeles, 1969, Sixteenth Edition), pp.CI, CII. Used by permission

114.	II Thessalonians 2:9-10.

115.	Judges 17:1-18:31.

116.	Deuteronomy 18:21-22, Jeremiah 14:14, Ezekiel 13:1-23, Matthew 7:15-23, I Thessalonians 5:20-22.

117.	Randy Frame, "Fund Raising: Did Oral Roberts Go Too Far?" Christianity Today, December 15, 2009 https://www.christianitytoday.com/ct/2009/decemberweb-only/151-21.0.html Accessed August 2019. Used by permission

118.	Kate Bowler, *Blessed: History of the American Prosperity Gospel* (Oxford University Press; Reprint Edition, 2013) p.129.

119.	Exodus 7:10-12, 8:5-7, Matthew 7:21-23, Acts 8:9-11.

120.	Matthew 24:23-24, II Thessalonians 2:9-10, Revelation 13:12-14.

121.	Hebrews 13:5-6, I Thessalonians 4:11-12, II Thessalonians 3:6-8

122.	Mark 4:19, II Kings 5:1-27.

123.	Leonardo Blair, The Christian Post, April 19, 2016 "Televangelist Paula White Hawks 'Resurrection Life' for $1,144 'Seed,'" https://www.christianpost.com/news/televangelist-paula-white-hawks-resurrection-life-1144-dollar-seed.html Accessed August 2019. Used by permission

124.   Michael Stone, "Religious Scholar Blasts Prosperity Gospel, Calls Joel Osteen a 'Charlatan,'" August 7, 2014, https://www.patheos.com/blogs/progressivesecularhumanist/2014/08/religious-scholar-blasts-prosperity-gospel-calls-joel-osteen-a-charlatan Accessed June 2019.

125.   Matthew 23:1-39, Mark 12:38-40, Luke 11:37-53, 16:14, 18:9-14, 20:45-47, John 3:1-21, 7:45-53.

126.   John Calvin, *Institutes of the Christian Religion*, Vol. 1 translated by Henry Beveridge, (Grand Rapids, MI: Wm. B. Eerdmans Publishing Co., 1957) p.648. Used by permission

127.   II Timothy 4:3-4 NIV.

128.   Dave Hunt and T. A. McMahon, *The Seduction of Christianity: Spiritual Discernment in the Last Days* (Oregon: Harvest House Publishers, 1985) p.213. Used by permission

129.   Kate Bowler, *Blessed: The History of American Prosperity Gospel* (New York: Oxford University Press, 2013), p.111.

130.   Lars Wilhelmsson, *The Gospel of Health, Wealth and Prosperity*, (Self-published) Preface p.6. Used with permission of the author.

131.   Exodus 20:17, I Corinthians 6:10.

132.   Colossians 3:5.

133.   Thomas Aquinas, "De Regimine Principum," in *St. Thomas Aquinas on Politics and Ethics*, On Kingship II. Translated and edited by Paul E. Sigmund, (New York: W.W. Norton & Company, 1988), p.3.

134.   Hebrews 13:5 Daniel 3:1-30.

135.   Roy McCloughry, "Basic Stott," Christianity Today www.christianitytoday.com/ct/2003/septemberweb-only/9-1-51.0.html Accessed August 2019. Used by permission

136.   Donald E. Gowan, "Wealth and Poverty in the Old Testament: The Case of the Widow, the Orphan, and the Sojourner," https://journals.sagepub.com/doi/abs/10.1177/002096438704100402 Accessed June 2019. Used by permission.

137.   I Timothy 6:10.

138.   Craig L. Blomberg, *Neither Poverty Nor Riches: Biblical Theology of Possessions*, New Studies in Biblical Theology (Leicester: Apollos, 1999) pp.17-18. Used by permission.

139.   Jeff Chu and David van Biema, "Does God Want You to Be Rich?" http://content.time.com/time/magazine/article/0,9171,1533448,00.html Accessed May 2019.

140.   Shayna L. Lear, "The Bankrupt Theology of the Prosperity Gospel," Prism Magazine, https://prismmagazine.org/that-you-may-prosper-in-all-things Accessed July 2019. Used by permission.

141.   Sean DeMars, "Do You Know What Your Missionaries Teach?! https://www.9marks.org/article/journaldo-you-know-what-your-missionaries-actually-teach/ Accessed February 2019. Used by permission.

142.   Rick Henderson, "The False Promise of the Prosperity Gospel: Why I Called Out Joel Osteen and Joyce Meyer,"https://www.huffpost.com/entry/osteen-meyer-prosperity-gospel_b_3790384, Accessed August 2018.

143.   Miguel Núñez, "Why has the Prosperity Gospel Prospered?" https://www.9marks.org/article/journalwhy-has-prosperity-gospel-prospered/ Accessed September 2018. Used by permission.

144.   Proverbs 22:22-23, Isaiah 3:14-15, Jeremiah 6:13, 8:10.

145.   John MacArthur, "Toxic Television: A Biblical Answer to the Prosperity Gospel, Part 1," https://www.gty.org/library/sermons-library/90-63M/toxic-television-a-biblical-answer-to-the-prosperity-gospel-part-1 Accessed November 2018. Used by permission.

146.   Micah 3:11 NIV.

147.   Lisa Withrow, "Success and the Prosperity Gospel: From Commodification to Transformation," Oxford Institute ofMethodist Theological Studies 2007: https://oimts.files.wordpress.com/2013/04/2007-6-withrow.pdf Accessed November 2018. Used with permission of the author.

148.   Ron Kubsch, ed. "A Statement on Prosperity Teaching," Lausanne Theology Working Group. 2010: http://www.christianitytoday.com/ct/2009/decemberweb-only/gc-prosperitystatement.html Accessed November 2018. Used by permission.

149.   Taken from *Telling the Truth: Evangelizing Postmoderns*, ed. by D. A. Carson © 2000, p.28, citing Ravi Zacharias "An Ancient Message, Through Modern Means to a Postmodern Mind." Used by Permission of Thomas Nelson. www.thomasnelson.com

150.   II Peter 2:10-19, 2:1, Jude 4.

151.   Lindsay Elizabeth, "Joyce Meyer Takes a Jab at the Prosperity Gospel, Denounces Her Past Beliefs In It," https://www.faithwire.com/2019/01/14/joyce-mehyer-takes-a-jab-at-the-prosperity-gospel-denounces-her-past-beliefs-in-it Accessed February 2019. Used by permission.

152. Leonardo Blair, "Televangelist Benny Hinn Admits Going Too Far with Prosperity Gospel in Wake Of Billy Graham's Death," The Christian Post, February 22, 2018,https://www.christianpost.com/news/televangelist-benny-hinn-admits-going-too-far-with-prosperity-gospel-in-wake-of-billy-grahams-death-219011 Accessed March 2018. Used by permission.

153. Randall Balmer, "Benny Hinn," in The Encyclopedia of Evangelicalism (Waco, TX: Baylor University Press, 2004) p. 336. Used by permission

154. Leah Marieann Klett, "Benny Hinn's Pastor Nephew Slams Prosperity Gospel, Urges 'Real Churches' to Say 'That is Not Christianity," The Gospel Herald Ministries, February 22, 2018,https://www.gospelherald.com/articles/71527/20171025/benny-hinns-pastor-nephew-slams-prosperity-gospel-urges-real-pastors.htm Accessed May 2018.

155. Taken from *Strange Fire: The Danger of Offending the Holy Spirit with Counterfeit Worship* 1st Edition by John F. MacArthur, © 2013, p.171. Used by permission of Thomas Nelson. www.thomasnelson.com

156. Kenneth E. Hagin, *The Midas Touch: A Balanced Approach to Biblical Prosperity,* (Tulsa, OK: Faith Library Publications, 2002) p.140.

157. Randall Balmer, *Encyclopedia of Evangelicalism* (Waco, TX: Baylor University Press, 2004) p.52. Used by permission

158. Christianity Today, "The Re-education of Jim Bakker," https://www.christianitytoday.com/ct/1998/december7/8te062.html Accessed May 2018. Used by permission

159. Randall Balmer, *Encyclopedia of Evangelicalism* (Waco, TX: Baylor University Press, 2004) p.59. Used by permission

160. AFP Relaxnews, "Vatican creates R1.6k eRosary to teach people to pray with their smartphones," Sunday Times, October 17, 2019,https://www.timeslive.co.za/sunday-times/lifestyle/2019-10-17-vatican-creates-r16k-erosary-to-teach-people-to-pray-with-their-smartphones/ Accessed October 2019.

161. Martin Luther, *Selections from His Writings*, ed. John Dillenberger (New York: Doubleday, 1961) p.97.

162. Paul G. Schervish and Keith Whitaker, *Wealth and the Will of God – Discerning the Use of Riches in the Service of Ultimate Purpose* (Bloomington, IN: Indiana University Press, 2010) p.137. Used by permission

163.   Taken from "Christianity in Crisis, The 21st Century" by Hank Hanegraaff © 2012 p.187. Citing Frederick Price, "Ever Increasing Faith." Used by permission of Thomas Nelson. www.thomasnelson.com

164.   Zechariah 9:9, Luke 9:58, II Corinthian 8:9, Philippians 2:6–8.

165.   Luke 2:7, 22-24, Leviticus 12:7-8.

166.   Exodus 21:32.

167.   Matthew 27:57-60.

168.   Matthew 10:9–10, Luke 8:1-3, 9:58.

169.   Luke 12:15, 16:13.

170.   I Corinthians 4:9-13, II Corinthians 4:16-18, 11:24-27, Hebrews 11:13-16, 26-38.

171.   II Corinthians 8:9, Philippians 2:6-11.

172.   Acts 18:1-3.

173.   Acts 20.33-35.

174.   Rob Perry, "The Rolls-Royce Gospel" https://salvationist.ca/articles/2009/02/the-rolls-royce-gospel Accessed May 2018. Used by permission.

175.   Luke 16:10-11, Proverbs 22:1

176.   Gary W. Smith, *Life Changing Thoughts: Thousands of Inspiring, Life-changing, and Humorous Thoughts* (Bloomington, Indiana: AuthorHouse, 2009) p.467. Charles Spurgeon, "Holding Fast the Faith" cited in Used by permission

177.   Acts 15, Galatians 2:10.

178.   Dieter Lührmann, *Galatians: A Continental Commentary* (Minneapolis: Fortress Press, 1992) pp.41-42. Used by permission

179.   II Corinthians 2:17.

180.   Acts 20:33-35, II Corinthians 2:17, I Thessalonians 2:5.

181.   Galatians 5:22-23, I Corinthians 12-14.

182.   Romans 14:17, 16:18, Philippians 3:19.

183.   Robert Murray McCheyne, "Robert Murray McCheyne Quotes", https://www.mcheyne.info/quotes/Accessed May 2018.

184.   I Timothy 3:3, 3:8, I Peter 5:2.

185.   Titus 1:1, II Timothy 3:2-4.

186.   Mark 4:18-19.

187.   Philippians 3:18-21 NKJV.

188.   Matthew 10:9-15, I Corinthians 9:1-14, II Timothy 2:6, Deuteronomy 25:4.

189.   II Corinthians 11:7-15.

190.   II Corinthians 2:17 NLT.

191.	Taken from *Life Application Study Bible Notes* by Tyndale House Publishers. Copyright © 1986, 1988, 1989, 1990, 1991, 1993, 1996, 2004. p.1974. Used by permission of Tyndale House Publishers, a Division of Tyndale House Ministries. All rights reserved.

192.	D.A. Carson, *When Jesus Confronts the World: An Exposition of Matthew 8–10*, (Grand Rapids, MI: Baker Publishing Group, 1987) p.125. Used by permission

193.	Matthew 26:6-13, I Corinthians 16:3-4, Romans 16:17-18, Philippians 3:17-19, Hebrews 13:17.

194.	Luke 19:1-10.

195.	Robert Booth, "Charity Commission Report Found Kingsway International Christian Center Lost Most of £5m Invested by Former Charlton Footballer Richard Rufus https://www.theguardian.com/world/2017/feb/12/kicc-kingsway-christian-centre-fraud-inquiry-richard-rufus Accessed March 2018. Courtesy of Guardian News and Media Ltd.

196.	John Piper, *Preparing for Marriage: Help for Christian Couples* (Revised and Expanded Edition), pp.18-19 Published for Desiring God by CruciForm Press (www.cruciformpress.com). Copyright © 2018 by Desiring God, Post Office Box 2901, Minneapolis, MN 55402. All rights reserved.

197.	Ecclesiastes 5:10-12 NIV.

198.	Isaiah 58:6-7, Luke 12:15-21, Acts 2:44-45, James 2:1-7, 5:1-6.

199.	I Corinthians 11:17-34.

200.	Hebrews10:34, 11:40.

201.	Luke 3:7-14, Deuteronomy 15:11, Acts 2-6, I John 3:17-18.

202.	Mark 10:28-30.

203.	Mark R. Gornik, "The Rich and the Poor in Pauline Theology," (Journal of Urban Mission: 9 September 1991), p.23. Used by permission

204.	William J. Larkin Jr., *Acts* (Downers Grove & Leicester: IVP Academic, 1995) p.83. Used by permission

205.	James 2:15-16.

206.	Craig L. Blomberg, *Neither Poverty Nor Riches: Biblical Theology of Possessions*, New Studies in Biblical Theology (Leicester: Apollos, 1999) p.155. Used by permission

207.	Jeremiah 22:13-17, Amos 4:1, Malachi 3:5, James 5:1-6.

208.	Philemon 10-19, Ephesians 6:5-9, Colossians 4:1.

209.	Luke 6:34, 14:12-14.

210.	Psalm 90:17, I Thessalonians 4:11-12.

211.	Proverbs 6:10-11, 10:4, 10:15, I Thessalonians 5:14, II Thessalonians 3:6-15, Ephesians 4:28.

212. I Timothy 5:3-9.

213. Exodus 22:21-24, Psalm 10:9-14, Job 29:11-17, Isaiah 10:1-2, Zechariah 7:10.

214. Proverbs 3:27-28, 21:13, 29:7, 31:20, Psalm 72:4, 82:3-4.

215. I Corinthians 9:9-12

216. Deuteronomy 6:7.

217. Matthew 7:12, 25:31-46, Luke 6:31.

218. Craig L. Blomberg, *Neither Poverty Nor Riches: Biblical Theology of Possessions*, New Studies in Biblical Theology (Leicester: Apollos, 1999) p.84. Used by permission

219. Exodus 21:1-11, Leviticus 19:9-10, Deuteronomy 15:1-11, 15:12-18

220. Job 31:24-28, Proverbs 29:7.

221. Acts 6:1-4.

222. I Thessalonians 4:11, Psalm 131:1-2.

223. I Corinthians 13:3.

224. Acts 6:1-7.

225. Tomika DePriest and Joyce Jones, "Economic Development through the Church," Black Enterprise, Vol. 27 No. 7, February 1997, p. 196https://www.questia.com/magazine/1G1-19051611/economic-deliverance-thru-the-church Accessed May 2018

226. Taken from *Proverbs*, by Kenneth T. Aitken, p.190 Copyright © 1986. Used by permission of Westminster John Knox Publisher

227. Proverbs 8:18.

228. Taken from *Leviticus* (Word Biblical Commentary) by John E. Hartley, ©1992, p.445 Used by permission of Thomas Nelson. www.thomasnelson.com

229. II Corinthians 8-9, 8:12.

230. Deuteronomy 16:16-17.

231. Exodus35-40.

232. I Chronicles 29:1-9.

233. Ezra 2:68-69.

234. Acts 11:28-30 II Kings 22:3-7.

235. I Timothy 6:7.

236. Proverbs 3:9-10.

237. George Macdonald, *3,000 Quotations from the Writings of George MacDonald* (Michigan: Fleming H. Revell, 1996), p.99. Used by permission

238. Luke 16:9-13, Acts 2:44-45, 4:32-35, Romans 12:8, 13, II Corinthians 9:5-13 Ephesians 4:28, I Timothy 6:17-19.

239. Acts 4:32-34, II Corinthians 8:1-2.

240. I Timothy6:17-19 NKJV.

241. Numbers 6:24-26.

242. I Chronicles 13:12-14.

243. Ecclesiastes 5:8-17.

244. John 9:1-41, II Corinthians 12:7-10.

245. Romans 4:13, Revelation 21-22.

246. Acts 5:12-42.

247. Craig L. Blomberg, *Neither Poverty Nor Riches: Biblical Theology of Possessions*, New Studies in Biblical Theology (Leicester: Apollos, 1999) p.36. Used by permission

248. II Timothy 1:5.

249. Exodus 20:12, Proverbs 20:20, Matthew 15:4-6, Mark 7:9-13, John 19:25-27, Romans 1:30, Ephesians 6:1-3; Colossians 3:20, I Timothy 5:3-8, II Timothy 3:2

250. Proverbs 13:11, Luke 14:28-32.

251. Hebrews 13:5 NIV

252. Luke 9:23-25, Matthew 10:16-20, Romans 8:17.

253. Jeremiah 23:1-8, Isaiah 9:6-7, I Corinthians 6:2, Ephesians 2:6, Revelation 2:26-27, 20:4.

254. Revelation 2:8-11, 3:14-22.

255. Matthew 23:27-28.

256. David A. deSilva, "The Social Setting of The Revelation to John: Conflicts Within, Fears Without," http://doc.uments.com/d-the-social-setting-of-the-revelation-to-john-conflicts-within.pdf Accessed May 2019. Used with permission of the author

257. Proverbs 30:8-9 NIV.

258. James 1:9-12.

259. I Timothy 6:6-8 NKJV.

260. Philippians 4:11-13 NKJV.

261. Matthew 19:16-30, Mark 10:17-31, Luke 18:18-30.

262. Ephesians 2:8-10.

263. Paul G. Schervich and Keith Whitaker, *Wealth and the Will of God – Discerning the Use of Riches in the Service of Ultimate Purpose*, (Bloomington, Indiana: Indiana University Press 2010) p.135 citing John Calvin, Commentaries (Sermon on Job 22:18–22). Used by permission

264. Colossians 3:1--4 NIV.

23:1-8

Ezekiel

7:19-20
13:1-23
16:49-50
36:1-37:28

Daniel

3:1-30

Hosea

2:8
8:4-6
13:4-8

Amos

3:3
4:1
6:4-6
6:12-13

Micah

3:11

Haggai

2:8

Zechariah

7:10
9:9
12-14

Malachi

3:5

Matthew

4:8-11
6:24
6:31-32
7:12
7:15-23
7:21-23

10:9-15
10:16-20
13:22
15:4-6
16:24-26
19:23
18:20
19:16-30
21:12-13
23:1-39
23:27-28
24:10-11
24:23-24
26:6-13
27:57-60
28:20

Mark

4:18-19
7:9-13
10:17-31
10:28-30
12:38-40
13:20

Luke

2:7
2:22-24
3:7-14
6:31
6:34
8:1-3
9:23-25
9:58
11:37-53
12:13-21
12:15-21
14:12-14
14:28-32
16:9-13
16:14
18:9-14
18:18-30
19:1-10
20:45-47

John

1:13
2:13-22

3:1-21
6:1-69
7:45-53
9:1-41
17:14
19:25-27

Acts

2:1-6:15
2:44-45
3:1-10
4:32-35
5:12-42
6:1-7
8:9-11
8:18-23
11:28-30
15:1-41
16:16-40
18:1-3
19:23-41
20:33-35

Romans

1:30
4:13
8:17
11:1-25
11:25-27
12:8, 13
14:17
16:17-18
16:25-27

I Corinthians

4:9-13
6:2
6:10
9:1-14
10:1, 10
11:17-34
11:24-27
12-14
13:3
16:3-4

II Corinthians

2:17

4:16-18
8:1-2
8:9
8-9
8:12
9:5-13
10:12-13
11:7-15
12:7-10

Galatians

1:6-9
2:10
3:1-14
5:22-23

Ephesians

1:3-12
1:9-12
2:6
2:8-10
3:20
4:28
6:1-3
6:5-9

Philippians

2:6-11
3:17-19
3:18-21
4:11-13

Colossians

1:26-27
2:4
3:1–4
3:5
4:1

I Thessalonians

2:5
4:11-12
5:14
5:20-22

II Thessalonians

2:1-3
2:9-10
3:6-15

I Timothy

3:3
3:8
3:16
4:1
5:3-9
5:23
6:6-8
6:6-11
6:17-19

II Timothy

1:5
2:6
3:1-5
3:12
4:3-4

Titus

1:1

Philemon

1:10-19

Hebrews

7:1-28
10:34
11:13-16, 26-38
11:24-26
11:40
13:5-6
13:17

James

1:9-12
2:1-7
2:15-16
4:3-4
5:1-6

I Peter

1:14-15
5:2

II Peter

2:1
2:3
2:10-19

I John

2:15
2:16-17
3:17-18

Jude

1:4

Revelation

2:8-11
2:26-27
3:14-22
13:8
13:12-14
13:16-18
17:8
20:4
21-22

BIBLIOGRAPHY

1. Aitken, Kenneth T., *Proverbs* (Louisville: Westminster John Knox Publisher, 1986)

2. Aquinas, Thomas. *St. Thomas Aquinas on Politics and Ethics.* Translated and edited by Paul E. Sigmund. (New York: W.W. Norton, 1988)

3. Asamoah-Gyadu, J. Kwabena *African Charismatics: Current Developments within Independent Indigenous Pentecostalism in Ghana*, (Boston: Brill Leiden, 2005)

4. Aulén, Gustaf *The Faith of the Christian* Church (Wipf & Stock Publishers, 2002)

5. Aune, David E. *Revelation 17—22*, Word Biblical Commentary Series (Nashville: Thomas Nelson, 1998)

6. Balmer, Randall H. *The Encyclopedia of Evangelicalism* (Waco, TX: Baylor University Press, 2004

7. Barnes, Sandra L. *Live Long and Prosper: How Black Megachurches Address HIV/AIDS and Poverty in the Age of Prosperity Theology* (New York: Fordham University Press, 2013)

8. Bauckham, Richard J. *2 Peter, Jude* (Waco: Word, 1983)

9. Blomberg, Craig L. *Neither Poverty Nor Riches: A Biblical Theology of Material Possessions*(NSBT 7; Grand Rapids: Eerdmans, 1999), 132

10. Blomberg, Craig L. *Neither Poverty Nor Riches – Biblical Theology of Material Possessions* (New Studies in Biblical Theology), Series Editor: D. A. Carson, Leicester: Apollos – an imprint of Inter-Varsity Press), 1999.

11. Bowler, Kate Bowler, *Blessed: History of the American Prosperity Gospel* Oxford University Press; Reprint Edition (2013)

12. Calvin, John. *Institutes of the Christian Religion*, translated by Henry Beveridge (Grand Rapids, Michigan: Eerdmans, 1957)

13. Calvin, John *Commentaries (Sermon on Job 22:18–22)* Trans. and ed. John King et al. Grand Rapids, Michigan: Baker Book House (1981)

14. D.A. Carson, *Telling the Truth:Evangelizing Postmoderns*,(Grand Rapids: Zondervan, 2000)

15. Carson, D. A. *When Jesus Confronts the World: An Exposition of Matthew 8- 10*, Grand Rapids: Baker; Leicester: IVP (1987)

16. Constable Thomas L. *Notes on Matthew* (studylight.org/com) 2019 Edition

17. Copeland Kenneth, *Our Covenant with God* (Fort Worth, TX: Kenneth Copeland Publications, 1996)

18. Farah, Charles Jr. *From the Pinnacle of the Temple: Faith or Presumption* (Plainfield, NJ: Bridge Logos Publishers, 1980)

19. Fee, Gordon D, *The Disease of the Health and Wealth Gospels* (Vancouver: Regent College Publishing, 2006), Kindle Edition

20. France RT, *The Gospel of Matthew.* The New International Commentary on the New Testament Series (Grand Rapids: Wm. B. Eerdmans Publishing Co., 2007)

21. Grudem Wayne, *Business for the Glory of God: The Bible's Teaching on the Moral Goodness of Business* (Illinois: Crossway Books, 2003)

22. Hagin, Kenneth E. *The Midas Touch: A Balanced Approach to Biblical Prosperity* (Faith Library Publications, 2002)

23. Hall Manly P., *Masonic, Hermetic, Qabbalistic and Rosicrucian Symbolical Philosophy* (Los Angeles, 1969, Sixteenth Edition)

24. Hanegraaff, Hank *Christianity in Crisis, The 21st Century* (Thomas Nelson, 2012)

25. Harrison, Milmon F. *Righteous Riches: The Word of Faith Movement in Contemporary African American Religion* (Oxford University Press, 2005)

26. Hartley, John E., *Leviticus* (Dallas: Word, 1992)

27. Hauerwas, Stanley, *Matthew.* (Brazos Theological Commentary, Grand Rapids: Baker, 2006)

28. Hengel, Martin *Property and Riches in the Early Church* (Fortress, 1974)

29. Hunt Dave and McMahon T. A., *The Seduction of Christianity: Spiritual Discernment in the Last Days* (Oregon: Harvest House Publishers, 1985)

30. Larkin, William J., Jr *Acts* (IVP: Leicester and Downers Grove, 1995)

31. Lincoln, C. Eric and Lawrence H. Mamiya, *The Black Church in the African-American Experience* (Durham: Duke University Press, 1990)

32. Luhrmann, Dieter, *Galatians: A Continental Commentary* (Minneapolis: Fortress, 1992)

33. Luther, Martin, *Selections from His Writings*, Edited by John Dillenberger (New York: Doubleday, 1961)

34. Lutzer Erwin, *10 Lies about God and the Truth that Shatter Deception*, (Grand Rapids: Kregel, 2009)

35. MacArthur, John F. *Strange Fire: The Danger of Offending the Holy Spirit with Counterfeit Worship* (Thomas Nelson, 2013) 1st Edition

36. Macdonald George, *3,000 Quotations from the Writings of George MacDonald* (Michigan: Fleming H. Revell, 1996)

37. McConnell, Dan R. *A Different Gospel: The Cultic Nature of the Modern Faith Movement*, Updated Edition Paperback (Hendrickson Publishers: 1994)

38. *New Living Translation Life Application Study Bible* (Illinois: Tyndale House Publishers, 2013)

39. Parsley, Rod *God's Answer to Insufficient Funds* (Canal Winchester: World Harvest Church, 1992)

40. Piper, John *Preparing for Marriage: Help for Christian Couples* Revised and Expanded Edition (Minneapolis: CruciForm Press, 2018)

41. Price Frederick K.C. *Living in the Realm of the Spirit* (Harrison House, 1989)

42. Schervich Paul G. and Whitaker, Keith *Wealth and the Will of God – Discerning the Use of Riches in the Service of Ultimate Purpose* (Bloomington: Indiana University Press, 2010)

43. Smith, Gary W. *Life Changing Thoughts: Thousands of Inspiring, Life-changing, and Humorous Thoughts*, (AuthorHouse, 2009)

44. Stegemann, Wolfgang, *The Gospel and the Poor* (Philadelphia: Fortress, 1984)

45. Tasker, R. V. G. *The Gospel According to St. Matthew: An Introduction and Commentary.* Tyndale New Testament Commentaries Series (Grand Rapids: Wm. B. Eerdmans Publishing Co., 1961)

46. Thumma, Scott, and Dave Travis, *Beyond Megachurch Myths: What We Can Learn From America's Largest Churches.* 1st ed. (San Francisco, CA: Jossey-Bass, 2007)

47. Wilhelmsson, Las *The Gospel of Health, Wealth and Prosperity* (Self-published)

48. Wuthnow Robert, *God and Mammon in America* (New York: The Free Press, 1994)

49. https://www.9marks.org 9Marks Journal

50. http://doc.uments.com/deSilva, David A. "The Social Setting of The Revelation to John"

51. biblicalstudies.gospelstudies.org.uk Africa Journal of Theology, Judith L. Hill, PhD Theology of Prosperity

52. https://www.equip.org/Christian Research Journal

53. https://journals.sagepub.comGowan, Donald E. (1987), "Wealth and Poverty in the Old Testament"

54. www.iodlj.zou.ac.zw/ejournal/index.php/journal/article/Zimbabwe Open University, International Open & Distance Learning Journal Volume 1 Issue 1

55. http://www.ijhcs.com/index.php/ijhcs/index International Journal of Humanities and Cultural Studies

56. https://bible.orgJones, David W. "The Bankruptcy of the Prosperity Gospel"

57. wilsonquarterly.com Randall Stephens, The Wilson Quarterly, Book Review

58. https://jofum.comJournal of Urban Mission, Mark R. Gornik

59. https://www.questia.com/magazine Black Enterprise Magazine

60. http://www.christianitytoday.comChristianity Today Magazine

61. Lermanet.org/scientologynews/latimes/Los Angeles Times

62. https://prismmagazine.org Shayna L. Lear, "The Bankrupt Theology of the Prosperity Gospel"

63. https://content.time.com/time/margazine/Jeff Chu and David van Biema, "Does God Want You to Be Rich?"

64. www.ukapologetics.net UK Apologetics

65. https://www.churchofjesuschrist.org/Elder Dallin H. Oaks "The Parable of the Sower"

66. https://www.gty.org MacArthur, John "Toxic Television"

67. http://interactive.creflodollarministries.org Creflo Dollar Ministries website

68. http://www.conradmbewe.com

69. http://www.gotquestions.org

70. https://albertmohler.com

71. http://studylight.org/com

72. http://www.charismamag.comJames Robison, "Another View of the Prosperity Gospel"

73. https://www.christianpost.com

74. https://www.patheos.com"Religious Scholar Blasts Prosperity Gospel, Calls Joel Osteen a 'Charlatan'"

75. https://www.huffpost.comRick Henderson, "The False Promise of the Prosperity Gospel"

76. https://oimts.files.wordpress.com Lisa Withrow, "Success and the Prosperity Gospel"

77. https://www.faithwire.com

78. https://www.gospelherald.comLeah Marieann Klett, "Benny Hinn's Pastor Nephew Slams Prosperity Gospel"

79. https://www.timeslive.co.zaSunday Times, "Vatican creates R1.6k eRosary

80. https://www.grassley.senate.gov/newsChuck Grassley, "Ministry Responses to Televangelist Review"

81. https://salvationist.ca Rob Perry "The Rolls-Royce Gospel"

82. https://www.mcheyne.infoRobert Murray McCheyne Quotes

ACKNOWLEDGMENTS

I thank God for my family and their patience when I needed all the time I could get to focus on this work – my wife, Florence, and our adventuresome son, Ariel Sly II; my all-weather friends, brothers, and Gospel musicians Pastor Tendai Faravadya and Elder Timothy Chingosho and their respective families. I also acknowledge Dr Tarwirei Kurisa and family for the prayers and encouragement.

My respects to all who have maintained orthodox Christianity particularly when writing or speaking about prosperity preaching – some of whom I have quoted in this book. I am grateful to God for the Doctrine of Christ Church: may we continue to grow in sound doctrine. May God give us the grace to walk the talk at God Cares Foundation. I am also appreciative of the board members of The Bibliocentric Institute – indeed the essence is defending the faith even in this formative stage of TBI. I am also appreciative of ministers of the Gospel who sacrificed time to critique and recommend the book: Dr Reuben van Rensburg, Professor Steve Zimmerman, Minister McKinley Caughman, Pastor Mbongeni Simelane, Bishop Mpambaniso and Pastor Ekkie Tepsupornchai. It was a blessing to correct the manuscript based on your apt feedback. Thank you Pastor Jim McClarty, not only for the Foreword but for finding time to go through the manuscripts I send you. It is pleasing to learn humility in ministry which you notably exemplify, Reverend Dean Skinner.

I am grateful to the hundreds, if not thousands, of church leaders that I have interacted with in relation to the subject-matter of this book. Even the few with opposing views enhanced my perspective. It was humbling to receive great reviews and literary advice from seasoned writers like Mark Baird, David Wentz and Bernard Levine. I am grateful as well to the publishing, editing, and marketing teams for a job well done. How can I forget wonderful and encouraging friends I found when I wondered into my unchartered waters requesting copyright permissions!

Now unto Him who can do immeasurably more than all we could ask or imagine, according to His power that is at work within us, be all the glory, honour, reverence, worship, and praise. God, the triune, holy, incomparable, and self-existent has indeed blessed us in the heavenly realms with every spiritual blessing in Christ. O the depth of the riches of the wisdom and knowledge of God! How unsearchable His judgements! How mysterious His methods!

www.ingramcontent.com/pod-product-compliance
Lightning Source LLC
Chambersburg PA
CBHW071912120726
48001CB00005B/1716